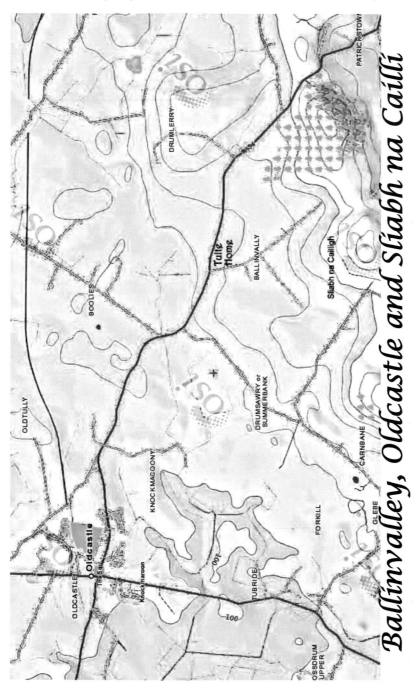

Ballinvalley, Oldcastle and Sliabh na Cailli

For my wife, May

These jottings, instigated by my daughter Helen, were written for

My children – Eamon, Mary, Margaret, Peter, Helen, Patrick, Anne, Finian, Brendan, and their families

My grandchildren – Donagh, Duana, Maeve, Alex, Ally, Anton, Emily, Peter, Patrick, Elena, Oisín, Ailbhe, Aoife, Rebecca, Sadhbh, Tiarnan, Rory, Seana, Fiachra, Isaac, Sinéad, Meera, Rohan, Dara, Muireann and Aibhín

My great-grandchildren – Milea and Colin

And those yet to come

I hope you enjoy these tales of simple, carefree days.

Jottings of a Country Boy

©2014 Peter Tuite

ISBN 978-1-78280-293-8

Published by Independent Publishers Network (www.ipubnet.co.uk)

JOTTINGS OF A COUNTRY BOY
1934-1948

BEGINNINGS

The Old Model T struggled up Caldergate Hill, rolled into the yard, bumped over a mound of concrete left by the builders, and we were home. We were my parents, Ned and Maggie (Fitzgibbon) Tuite, siblings Eddie, Oliver (Olo), Michael, Bridget (Dilly), Pat, me, and baby Maeve. All the worldly possessions of the Tuite family also fitted into the crib of the truck. The parents and the baby were in the cab, the rest of us riding to the rear in the crib with the few bits and pieces.

It was 1937, and we were taking possession of a new Land Commission house on about forty acres of fertile land in Ballinvalley, a townland two miles out of Oldcastle. A Land Commission house was a house built by order of and at the expense of a Government department of that name. The Commission had the responsibility of removing ownership of large estates from mostly colonists, and dividing the land among the natives. The Irish Government recouped its outlay by means of a sixty year annuity payable by us. The compensation paid to the landowners was funded by the British Treasury, and when De Valera decided to renege on repayment in 1932, the British stopped imports of agricultural products. This was the beginning of the Economic War which lasted until 1938. Ireland ground to a halt.

The move to Ballinvalley is my first clear memory of my young days. I was born in 1934 when the effects of the Economic War were being deeply felt. According to my Dad you could buy a calf for two shillings and sixpence (Euro 12 cents). My place of birth was originally the home of the governor of the WW1 German Prisoner of War camp in Oldcastle, which had been a garrison town. This camp had closed down shortly after the war, towards the end of 1918. In 1934 our family were tenants there. Often, when engaging in one-upmanship with my peers as young lads tend to do, I used to boast that I was born in a Prisoner of War camp. They generally found this difficult to match. According to Dr Philip O'Connell, (Riocht na Midhe Vol.111, No 3), the name 'Oldcastle' refers to an early castle from the period 1172-86 built by the Norman Tuites, so the Tuite name has a very long association with the area. The Camp was not much more than a stone's throw from the site of the old castle.

My family had been on the move fairly frequently in the period before my arrival. My older siblings (I was the 6th surviving) had lived in Newcastle, a townland of Oldcastle, before taking up residence in my birthplace. When I was a toddler we lived in Millbrook, close to O'Reilly's mill which was powered by water from the River Inny. When I was a bit bigger I remember going to the mill with my Dad to get oats cracked and maybe rolled (for porridge). Sadly, the mill is no longer in operation.

OTHER ABIDING EARLY MEMORIES

Being tall enough to be able to look into the dresser drawers.

Being forced to wear girl's drawers. I was so upset that it is still a searing memory. I screamed, I yelled, I banged my head off a door until eventually my Mother had to concede and remove them. I imagine that I was about three or four at the time.

In 1938/9 being in the back of the old Model T Ford with a number of my siblings and young neighbours on the way to a football match. The Model T had limited pulling power and gears. When we came to rise in the road of any duration the older fellows had to jump out and push.

Around age four, going one hot summer Sunday with the family to Lough Sheelin. I was so anxious to get to the water that I outran my siblings, dashed straight into deep water and had to be pulled out spluttering but undaunted.

Tuite Home, Ballinvalley

PLACE

BALLINVALLEY (BAILE AN BHEALAIGH)

The Irish name indicates that Ballinvalley was a 'town or homestead of the way or road' and indeed according to Dr O'Connell, there was an ancient roadway from Sliabh na Callaigh to Breiffne (Cavan). It passed close to St Patrick's Well in Boolies. Ballinvalley was two miles from Oldcastle and about a mile across the hill to Loughcrew estate, the home of the Naper family, which at one time owned the town and the whole countryside around there, as had the Tuites and the Plunketts before them. The Napers were Cromwellian settlers who took over from the Plunketts, Saint Oliver Plunkett's family, and the Tuites.

There used to be hardly a tree in sight in this area until my father started to plant some. It was all stone walls, some of them at least four feet wide and almost all five to six feet high. There were obviously a lot of stones and rock in the land before their removal helped create the very fertile, open farmland that is now there. In my time, some of the walls had openings at ground level to enable small animals, sheep and goats, to move from field to field. Sheep passes, I think they were called. The adjoining townland, Boolies, has some of the finest examples of these.

I demolished a one metre section of a low version of such a stone wall on my way in to the town on my First Communion morning. I headed off on my own for the service, nicely dressed and sparkling clean with a sixpence clutched in my little hand. As I was passing by Flood's Lane something attracted my attention in the field. I stretched over the wall to have a look and the sixpence slipped out of my hand and disappeared into the wall. Frantically, stone by stone, I reduced the level of the wall until I reached bare earth. Alas, the sixpence was not to be found! I left behind me a one metre gap in the wall, as I rushed off to the church. I was, to put it mildly, a dishevelled oddity among my fellow first communicants. On the way home I did try to repair the wall but it was not quite up to the standard of the rest of it. Every time I passed that section of the wall over the years it reminded me of the loss of my sixpence, but I have no recollection of the ceremony.

A Sheep Pass and Stile in Boolies – photo courtesy of David Sheridan

THE LOUGHCREW CAIRNS

Ballinvalley is an interesting area, being on the periphery of the world-famous Loughcrew Cairns, the largest passage grave complex in Ireland, dating from 3,500BC. There are remains of burial chambers spread out over three hilltops – Carnbane East, Carnbane West and Patrickstown, collectively known as Sliabh na Caillí or Sliabh na Callaigh. We lived closest to the principal hill, Carnbane East, which is also individually known as Sliabh na Callaigh. Locally we called the hill 'The Sturracheen', a word that refers to the pimple point on top of the hill – Irish *'Stoiricín' or 'Starracáin'*. The Sturracheen is just short of three hundred meters high. What we called 'the heap of stones' on the top of it – the Passage grave Cairn T – is a megalithic cairn to rival Newgrange. At sunrise on the Spring and Autumn equinoxes, a beam of light illuminates the backstone of the burial chamber.

Cairn T on The Sturracheen seen from Ballinvalley. Photo 'Ballinvally stone circle' ©
Copyright Kieran Campbell, licensed for reuse under Creative Commons Licence.

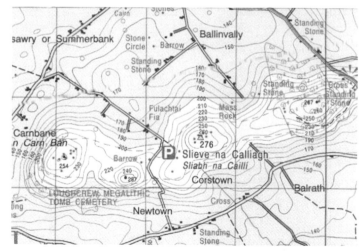

The hills and valleys are dotted with stone circles and individual rocks carved in situ (Rock Art). One of the stone circles was on our land. In addition to the megalithic art on the stones of the burial mounds, Ballinvalley holds fifteen of the seventeen known examples of Rock Art in Meath (Eogan, Riocht na Midhe, Vol 22, 2011). Five thousand years ago Ballinvalley must have been a much more important place than it appears to be now!

BAREFOOT THROUGH THE FIELDS

There was wonderful freedom growing up in Ballinvalley. We walked to school and that four or five miles a day for all our school years was very important for our long-term health, as well as keeping us in touch with nature. Sometimes we took 'shortcuts' across the fields, especially in summer when we were in our bare feet. We observed the behaviour of birds and animals, plucked damsons from the hedges, caught trout in the Inny, and probably extended the four miles by 50% in any one day. Talking about birds, on our way to school we used to watch out for and listen to the many woodpeckers which frequented Sheridans' wooded lawns in the 1940s. There are none to be seen or heard now, although I read recently (2013) that woodpeckers are being seen and heard again in certain parts of Ireland. There were owls around farmhouses too, and in the odd place where there were a few trees.

It was customary in those days to go barefoot on April 1$^{st.}$ Our parents would not allow us to do so beforehand but we would do it earlier by removing our boots outside the gate and slinging them over our shoulders. Apart from Sundays and special occasions, we would not take to the boots again until All Souls. Someone unfamiliar with country life at that time might assume that we went barefoot because we had no footwear, especially as our townie peers always wore shoes. We were always well shod when we needed footwear, normally boots a size too big, to allow for growth. These would be treated before wearing with a mass of studded nails in the heels and toes to prolong life. These studs were also brilliant for the slides on frosty days.   I remember my brothers Olo, Michael, Pat and I – all barefoot – going up to Matt Reilly's on Halloween to collect hazelnuts. ('Matt Reilly's' was one of the Loughcrew hills where Matt, who was a politician, had winter grazing). It was dusk when we started home and we were glad to get there because there was frost building up on the grass and we were feeling it on our feet.

The Loughcrew hills were an important activity trap for us growing up. The hill was always teeming with rabbits, and we kids were forever futilely chasing them. My father advised us to shake a pinch of salt on their tails and they would wait up for us. It probably took a couple of innocent years for us to lose faith in that message!

Salting the Rabbit by Rohan Mulcahy Tuite age 5

That was Dad's solution for catching plover as well. Plover, both the Pilibín (Green Plover) and the smaller Golden Plover, were fey creatures and they scattered if you got within a hundred yards of them. In those days, before all the drainage took place, there was a lot of surface water everywhere in winter and we had wild geese in droves in 'the bottoms', an adjoining field. We used to throw the odd sheaf of oats to them. I don't know if the conditions prevailing then were also more favourable to the plover than now, at any rate there are now no visiting plover in the area. There were heron, snipe, duck, curlew, all now as you might say, drained away.

Gavin's Rock, just down from the peak of Sliabh na Callaigh, (Hill of the Witch or Hag) was an outcrop of rock facing south over the flat plains of northwest Meath. It formed a cliff about 30 feet high, and just down from the top was a little cave or crevice concealed by a shrub. I was a voracious reader from the time I first learned to read – sitting on Uncle Mickey's knee on one of his visits. (Mickey was helping me to read a children's book, and after a few minutes, *click*, I could read fluently. It was as if a veil had been removed from my understanding).

Because reading was well-nigh impossible in the house due to the noisy siblings and because, if I were truthful, the constant calls to "do this, do that,' interfered with it, I used to sneak off to my little cave and read to my heart's content. From there I remember once seeing just below me a fox and three young cubs disporting themselves in complete ignorance of my close presence. Nice!

Peter watching the foxes play by Elena Tuite Andropoulos (16)

An Maidrín Rua
An maidrín rua, rua, rua, rua, rua,
An maidrín rua 'tá gránna,
An maidrín 'na luí sa luachair,
'Gus barr a dhá chluas in airde.

OUR STONE CIRCLE

The stone circle on our land, now no longer in existence (above ground anyway), deserves a more detailed mention. Part of the Loughcrew Cairns complex, and around 5500 years old, it was a circle of huge rocks, all about five to six feet high and two to three feet wide by about a foot and a half thick. The diameter to my eight or nine year old eyes, looked as if it could be 100 yards, but in reality about half that, I suppose. In the centre of the circle were other little grass mounds. The reason that I am unsure of the dimensions is that it was destroyed in the early 1940s during the war. This had nothing to do with the war, it was done on the advice of the Antiquarian Society, which had been digging there for some time and had removed some artefacts. One of those, a large stone, five or six feet high with beautiful Megalithic writing is now housed in the National Museum in Dublin. A notice on it identifies it as having been removed from the land of Edward Tuite of Ballinvalley. It used to be in the main foyer, but it is now in storage.

A Loughcrew Stone Circle

The ancient stone circle was uprooted by Paddy Mack, our farm labourer. Paddy worked for us for many years. (In the thirties this was for a guinea a week and his food. This was the minimum wage for agricultural workers). Paddy was a little man, not much more than five feet tall, but incredibly strong for his size. He used to display his strength by lifting hundredweight bags of potatoes with his teeth!

Anyway, when the Antiquarian Society said they were finished, my father said, "What am I going to do with it now, it's in the middle of the field, neutralising an acre of good land?" They told him to dig big holes undermining the rocks, topple the rocks into them and bury them. That is what Paddy Mack spent an autumn and winter doing, to the effect that there is now no evidence of the underlying historical treasure. The Antiquarian Society's advice was a sad reflection on the attitude at the time to our national heritage. The photograph below is of one of the buried rocks brought to the surface by my brother Olo while ploughing was in progress in the early seventies. It is in storage in the national museum. (Photo courtesy of Nessa O'Connor in the National Museum).

Stone given to the National Museum in the 70s by Ned Tuite

In the early eighties, knowing roughly where these rocks were buried, I tried to dig one out with Olo's permission, and remove it from Ballinvalley to my new garden in Dunshaughlin. It was about six feet tall, of slightly rounded rectangular shape, with, unusually, a short neck and a round head on which the Ogham writing was inscribed. Fortunately, as it turned out, the old JCB that I had hired to do the job was unable to lift it, and it was returned to mother earth and reburied. My brother Olo, whose land it was, had been watching uneasily from the sidelines – out of respect for ancient sacred monuments rather than for any concern that the field was being damaged. I could see that he was greatly relieved when the project was aborted.

As for Paddy Mack, years later he upped stakes and went off to Coventry. I have met him only once since my boyhood days, in the 70s I think. We were at a funeral in Oldcastle, and after warm greetings, Paddy pulled a fistful of English pounds out of his pocket and said, "See that, Peter. *That's* a week's wages in Coventry. That is what I earned in all the years I worked in Ballinvalley". It had been a courageous move to emigrate in his late middle years and the vibrancy of his sense of achievement made a lasting impression on me.

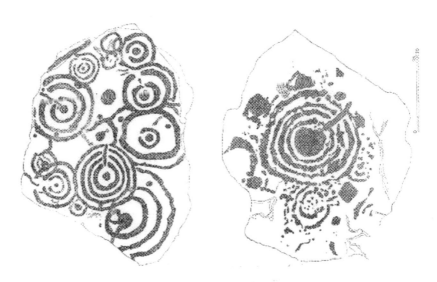

Ballinvalley Rock Art

THE HAG'S CHAIR

One of the large rocks forming a circle around 'the heap of stones' on top of the central hill is known as the 'Hag's Chair'. At one time the face of this five-and-a-half-thousand year old 'heap of stones' (Cairn T) was a spectacular white, as the outer ring was clad with milky quartz, 'grian cloch' in Irish (sunstone). Since one can see sixteen, perhaps eighteen counties from it, it is safe to assume that it was also visible from many of them. It must have been a shining beacon to ancient inhabitants! Some of that quartz was still scattered about the cairn in the nineteen thirties and forties but you would struggle to find a bit now. Visitors continuously carried pieces away with them over many years until there was none left. I and my siblings took some, mostly because we could light a fire by striking two pieces together. We called it 'flint'.

As we grew up the traditional belief was that the heap of stones was built up over the centuries by pilgrims who carried a stone up the hill as a mark of respect to the dead interred there. On inspection the Hag's Chair looks like a Mass Rock, since it has a cross etched in the stone like an altar. I have a dim memory of attending a Mass there as a wee fellow. We used to play around the Hag's Chair. We sat on it and gazed down on Ballinvalley, on Oldcastle, and off in the distance Lough Sheelin and Lough Ramor.

Tradition has it that the Cailleach Garavogue, (or the Cailleach Bheara) used to sit on her chair and watch the stars. She was a fabled creature of the distant past, able to renew her powers from the endless forces of nature. This 'monster woman' once ruled the area. But to rule over all of Ireland she needed to drop an apron-full of rocks on each of the three peaks of Sliabh na Callaigh, jumping from one peak to the next. She succeeded with the first two peaks, but failed on the last one and fell to her death, leaving a trail of passage tombs and burial mounds scattered all over the area.

Pat, Cella, Maeve, Dilly, Willie and Andrew Tuite on The Hag's Chair c.1952

Jonathan Swift visited Sliabh na Callaigh in the seventeen hundreds and afterwards wrote the following ditty about the witch:

Oldcastle, Co. Meath

Determined now her tomb to build,
Her ample skirt with stones she filled,
And dropped a heap on Carnmore;
Then stepped one thousand yards, to Loar,
And dropped another goodly heap;
And then with one prodigious leap
Gained Carnbeg; and on its height
Displayed the wonders of her might.
And when approached death's awful doom,
Her chair was placed within the womb
Of hills whose tops with heather bloom.

Jonathan Swift, c. 1720

Walking from the Sturracheen to Carnbane West 2013

THE RIVER INNY (AN EITHNE)

Arising in Matt Reilly's hill and flowing through our neighbour, Pee Farrelly's land, then into 'Mack's Field' (our historic heritage field), and then on, would you believe it, into the Atlantic, via Lough Ree on the Shannon, this little stream gave us many pleasurable hours. The old Irish name for this river was An Eithne, after "a fabled goddess in Celtic or pre-Celtic mythology" (Riocht na Midhe 111 No1, 1963, P11). The stretch of it that was ours had a nice shallow flow of two to three inches. That is where we learned to swim. Really!

Tennyson might have been there, the description in his poem The Brook putting into clever words the scene which we witnessed in Ballinvalley.

I come from haunts of coot and hern,
I make a sudden sally
And sparkle out among the fern,
To bicker down a valley.
(Alfred, Lord Tennyson)

Come sunny days in March/April, the urge to swim was strong, and off we would go to Mack's to create our own swimming pool. This we did by digging up scraws (Irish 'scraith', a sod dug up from a field), and damming the mouth of a bridge until the water flowed over it. We then had a little pool about twenty feet long by five wide with a depth ranging from 4ft at the bridge to 2ft upstream. We could dive into it and swim to our hearts' content. Wasn't it cold? It didn't bother us then, even though it was basically spring water from the hill. A bonus was that, as the water supply was cut off downstream, the flapping trout were easy prey.

When we got a bit bigger we used to walk several miles in the river dragging a bran bag with us, and shepherding trout into it. The bran bag (a large, woven bag for transporting bran) had a circle of bull wire keeping the mouth open. It was a deadly trap. The stream, of course, by the time it reaches Oldcastle two miles away, is a river with two-foot-deep pools, so the size of the trout was much greater than upstream in Mack's field. Once, when I was home on holidays from London, my younger brothers Willie and Andrew and I dragged a bran bag all the way to Oldcastle without catching a single trout. We learned afterwards that the Fisheries Board had only a few days before travelled the upper reaches of the Inny with stun guns and removed all the fish to Lough Sheelin. Lough Sheelin, of course, is a well-known trout lake which offers exciting fishing in Mayfly season.

My brother Pat became a keen fisherman at an early age. He preferred legal fishing with rod and line. Because of difficulty in waking up in the mornings he devised a novel silent alarm clock in collaboration with a friend with whom he went fishing: He tied a fishing line to his big toe and cast the line out the window. The next morning all his friend had to do was to tug on the line to get Pat up.

After Oldcastle, the Inny meanders westwards towards Lough Sheelin via Castlecor and Mountnugent. It exits the lake at the other end, flowing under The Bridge of Finea. From there it wanders over the countryside through Lough Kinale, and on from there to the Streete/Lismacaffrey area, bypassing Granny Fitzgibbon's home.

Lough Derravaragh is the next lake to receive its ever-increasing riches, a mystical lake that inspired much storytelling concerning the mythical Children of Lir. After touching the boundaries of Abbeyshrule it heads for Pallas, the birthplace of Oliver Goldsmith. By the time it reaches the

Shannon the Inny is a significant addition to the waters of the mighty Shannon.

The River Inny near Ballymahon, Co Longford, photo courtesy of Cooney's Hotel

It is interesting to consider that the Loughcrew Hills may not only have put us, in Ballinvalley, beyond the Pale, but also that they were a watershed, diverting our water the long journey to the Atlantic in the West, away from the shorter journey eastwards to the Irish Sea. Only four miles away, the Blackwater meanders eastwards through the Meath plains to join the Boyne at Navan, and thence into the Irish Sea.

Another of our fields was in 'The Bottoms', a low-lying area that had its own little tributary of the Inny, fed from an underground spring. In the area of this stream there was a plentiful supply of blue clay. This is malleable, and we sometimes spent long periods digging it up, hauling it up to the yard and setting up a pottery bench. The resultant cups, eggcups, teapots, jugs etc. would not have graced Harrods, but we had many happy hours making them.

One time I was crossing a wall on my way down to this field. As I jumped down, the tail of my overcoat caught on a big stone on top of the wall and pulled it down on to my head. The blood gushed. We used to remove horns from bullocks with a saw – we called it 'sculling'. If you have ever seen a bullock being sculled too close to the beast's head, you would have seen blood spraying from the wound; jets of blood rising up in the air and falling back down drenching its head. That is what I imagined my head to be like as I ran back to the house in fear of dying on the spot! When my poor mother saw my bloody head *she* nearly died! There was no permanent damage (?), although I still have a slight depression at the point of impact.

THE LAKES

There is a semicircle of lakes around Oldcastle: Lough Ramor in the North East, at its nearest point to Ballinvalley not more than four miles away; Lough Sheelin in the North West, about eight miles away and Lough Lene in the West, about ten miles away. In between, there is a smaller lake called Lough Bawn and an even smaller one in Loughcrew. They are all beautiful, all teeming with fish, and all pretty well deserted most of the time. We have a long way to go in developing our leisure industry, getting the capital in to create facilities around the lakes, around Sliabh na Callaigh and Oldcastle itself.

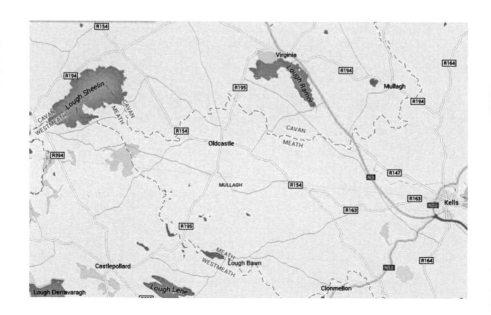

Pat and Peter on Lough Ramor c.1948

In the early forties, Pat and I spent many days on Lough Ramor on hired boats. At that time there were numerous boats for hire, there was a diving board, and there were many people on the Virginia side at weekends. (There are no facilities there now. People's habits have changed radically since those leisurely days, it seems).

Both of us were fit and we sometimes rowed the whole length of the lake and back again, a distance of over ten miles. There are so many beautiful islands on it and the shorelines are so pretty that it is a mystery that there are not more recreational activities there. The river Blackwater enters the Lough Ramor at Virginia and exits it at the Nine Eyed Bridge to continue on to Navan where it joins the Boyne.

Lough Sheelin, into which the Inny flows, is not so spectacularly beautiful, but it has other virtues. The water is clear, whereas that in Lough Ramor is a boggy brown; as a trout fishing lake it has an international reputation and it has a sandy shoreline in places, which encourages swimming. The bridge of Finea, made famous by Percy French, is located by the shore beyond Mountnugent. Until I got a damaging infection there in 1949, Lough Sheelin was one of my favourite places.

I got scabies from swimming there in the summer, just before returning to St Finian's boarding school for second year. The intensive pig farming which had developed near the lake and in that area of Cavan had polluted the lake and the local underground springs. This infection had unwarranted serious consequences for me arising from negligent medical attention. Because of lack of sleep from the untreated night time itching, my eyes deteriorated to the extent that within six to eight weeks I could not read the classroom blackboards, my attention span shortened and my concentration deteriorated. I fell badly behind in classroom and study. Worst of all, my confidence was shattered.

My mother came to see me after about ten weeks. After nearly fainting at the sight of me she called the President down and spurred him into action with some strong words spoken with feeling. With proper care I recovered physically within a month but psychological scars remained. It took me almost a year to get back to myself. If I go to Lough Sheelin now it is only to look and come away, although I used to cycle down to the Finea end of the lake during school holidays to meet up with my friend Tom Brady and to enjoy his mother's soda bread. She would have it hot out of the pot oven for me when she knew beforehand that I was coming. She was one of the many lovely, kind women that I had the happiness to encounter during my boyhood wanderings.

Lough Lene became a popular swimming place for youngsters from Oldcastle, Collinstown and Delvin after the pollution of Lough Sheelin. It has lovely clear and clean water and a raft-like structure about thirty yards offshore for resting on or diving off. During the warm days of haymaking Pat and I would hop on our bicycles as soon as we could quit the hay field and head off to this lake for a cooling swim. (Of course we were just as hot on our return after the twenty mile round trip). It could become quite crowded on Sundays. About twenty of us young teenagers, boys and girls, from around the area did a lifesaving course there once. It was a great social activity as well as an opportunity to acquire a useful skill.

Lough Derravaragh, located a little way beyond Lough Lene, is famous for the mythical swan children of Lir. It is a magical lake to look at as one passes it by on the Oldcastle to Mullingar road. It was easy to imagine the sad swans gliding along gracefully, in deathly silence in their ethereal world. But there was never to our minds a sense of the evil presence of Aoife.

Lough Ramor *by JoeBoy75*

The River Inny by Dara Reilly Tuite age 2

The River Inny by Meera Reilly Tuite age 6

FAMILY

DAD

My father, Ned Tuite, was a "dacent man", as quoted by many of his customers and friends. During the war the truck was off the road, and he had to revert to the horse-drawn sprung van, and limit his dealing to small animals, calves, sheep and pigs. He would go to a fair in, say, Swadlinbar, up towards the northern boundary of Cavan, perhaps 40 miles away. He would take animals there, starting off at around 2am, sell them,

and return that evening with other animals, normally calves. He was always on the lookout for veal calves for Jewish customers in Dublin, and he was occasionally successful in getting some. I met these customers once or twice immediately post-war. They were very sombre gentlemen with faces as long as their beards. They always ignored me, which was quite off-putting, but all was forgiven because they were so anxious to get the calves that they paid the asking price without haggling.

Dad had his regular clients for calves, and during the next few days after a fair he drove around the parish and beyond selling them. Occasionally, if a calf he had sold previously had not survived, he replaced it free of charge. I used to travel around with him during holiday time, and they were educational days – more so, I dare say, than school. I listened in to negotiations, soaking in the wisdom and decency and the humour of ordinary country folk. Dad also had regular clients among the landed Protestants. They never questioned or quibbled at the premium price.

Jottings of a Country Boy

I have always had a deep appreciation of the dedicated way Dad went about providing for a family of eleven children. An example: I have clear memories of the hardship involved in doing a 70/80 mile round trip in winter in an open cart. To prepare for the journey, my father heated a few wisps of hay in the oven for the wellingtons or the boots. He was a great fan of 'Lotus' boots which were comfortable and water proof and which had to be sourced from London. Keeping the feet warm was impossible in frosty conditions, but the hay helped. He would get a couple of hours sleep and some of us would stay up. At perhaps 1.30am, we would load the van with the animals before calling him. The horse would have frost nails, and Dad as much clothes as he could wrap around him. Off they would go into the frosty night. The horse, Bob, was a great goer. He seemed to be able to trot along briskly all day. He was also 'snappy' and one had to be careful not to get one's face too close to him. One evening Dad and I were out in the barn looking at the stock, it must have been winter. As we passed Bob's stable Dad noticed that the hay had been pulled from the manger on to the ground. "Hop in there and put the hay back". I hopped. As I raised my head in replacing the hay I got too close to Bob. Snap! The cut on my lip required stitching and I was just thankful that he hadn't removed my nose. The scar is still visible.

Bob

The four to five hour journeys would not be pleasant. During the course of the morning, Dad would do his selling and buying, and then head back as early as possible in order to get home before sunset. Despite the hardship, he seemed to get some satisfaction from his calling, especially as he enjoyed bantering.

Fortunately he did not drink, and we never had to witness the horse bringing him home, something not unusual for some of his friends and competitors!

He was a very affable man but I do not remember ever having a real conversation with him. Oh, there were desultory conversations, like: "I've changed my job, Dad". "Didn't you have a good job"? "Yes". Well, y'auld eejit"! There was always an understated humour in these brief conversations as my father didn't take himself that seriously, but he obviously had anxieties about change!

He used to read the paper to us in the evenings and start discussions, always brief, on the subject matter. His curiosity about everything was almost obsessive and for a man of his time his knowledge level was well above the average of those who had finished school at fourteen, as he had. He had only one strong view about politics – avoid the subject! He never allowed us to know what party he voted for, but we suspected that it was Fine Gael as he read The Irish Independent rather than The Irish Press, a Fianna Fáil paper. He claimed that he had seen brother kill brother in 'the Troubles' and he did not want to see us get enmeshed in that kind of madness.

Dad had a light touch dealing with us. When we misbehaved (for example by going on a day-long walkabout without informing them), we were sent up to bed. In anticipation of this, Pat would push me in ahead of him and position himself on the stairs ready for a quick getaway, leaving only me exposed to whatever punishment was coming. The cane would come out on these occasions, and although Dad only ever swished it close to us, we were still scared, until one day I looked back and saw him turning away, grinning.

Dad and Mam
Edward Tuite and Margaret Fitzgibbon (Wedding photo 1924)

MAM

This is a page for superlatives. My mother, Maggie, died young after seventeen pregnancies. The first child, Noel, died at age two, and eleven children survived. Detailed memories are clouded in the mists of time, but one thing stands out: we were all enveloped in her love, a self-sacrificing love which was quiet and certain. I can never think of my mother without the feeling of how unfair life was for her and most women until relatively recently. Although she would not regard it as such, she was burdened with too many children, a matter over which she had no control, even if the church influence was not brought to bear. Quite apart from that, life was hard in the Ireland of the 1930s, 40s and 50s. The economic war of the 1932-1938, allied to worldwide economic depression, set the country back radically. Then the war followed closely, depriving the country, not only of raw materials, foodstuff, fuel and other necessities, but also of many of its young people, as they took the boat in their thousands, mostly to replace the British soldiers going off to war. A half a million Irish emigrated to Britain during World War II. Our future was being exported (as was I) until the mid-sixties, when we finally began to see the prospect of a better one at home. If there was any good coming out of this situation, it was confined to the emigrants' remittances, which were in fact lifesavers for many. We also benefited from emigrants' remittances from America. At one time, I'm not sure if it was during or after the war, the government brought in a measure to exchange emigrants' remittance dollars at seven shillings and sixpence instead of the standard five shillings, presumably to encourage further remittances.

So there was little money, and that was always a worry, but at least we had the basic necessities of life: plenty of good, simple food, adequate clothing and shelter. We had our own horses, which we broke in ourselves, cart and trap, and one bicycle, so transport was not a problem. Time – there was plenty of that, so a two-day journey that can now be done in a couple of hours was not a problem either. Our birthday presents were hugs from our mother ("The cow didn't calve"), and that is all we wanted or expected. We had a very pragmatic outlook on life.

Dad was in the background doing a good job in providing for us. Mam was in the trenches every day, keeping her brood accepting, indeed happy. She washed all the clothes out of a barrel of rainwater, with vigorous use of soap and a scrubbing board, and there were no throw-away nappies then. She often had Mrs Willis from Knockbrack to help her, especially around times when she was giving birth. Mam cooked and baked and scraped and wore herself out, always cheerful, very often singing. She had a lovely voice,  and a fondness for Delia Murphy's songs. *The Spinning Wheel* and *Down by the Sally Gardens* are two whose lyrics I still remember.

Ten of the eleven of us emigrated, and Mam wrote religiously to all of us. Over the years she had some health problems necessitating long hospital stays. An abiding memory of her is the day I first saw her after such a stay. I was five or six, having spent months staying with Granny Tuite in The Tanyard. I wasn't too sure that it was my mother, but when she opened her arms to me with an expression full of emotion and love, I dashed into them, and there and then shed all the anxieties of the past few months in a motherless home. No bad reflection on Granny who was brilliant, but she wasn't my mother!

Summer 1926 Kathleen, Noel & Maggie Tuite

Jottings of a Country Boy

My mother, as far as I can gather, spent her young days as a servant in Rotherams, agents for the Naper Estates. The Rotherams were extensive landowners in their own right, owning outright, or leasing from the Napers, more than three thousand acres. This land stretched almost continuously from Tubride to Dromone.

It was, I suppose, from this anglicised environment that Mam pronounced some words with a 'posh' accent. The only one that now comes to mind is 'hames', which we in and around Oldcastle pronounced 'hams'. We used to laugh at our mother's 'haymes'! A hames, in case you don't know it, is a contraption with hooks, which is attached to a horse's collar. The pulling chains are attached to the hooks. The phrase 'making a hames' of something is associated, apparently because if you put the hames on upside down (easy to do) the result is a mess.

UNCLES AND AUNTS

Tanyard Tuites c.1910 – Bill, Johnny, Eddie; Lillie, Delia, Pee, Mickey, Kathleen (baby), Bridget (née Hayden), William & Packy

My uncles and aunts were very important to me when I was growing up. They always made time for me and my siblings. They were good humoured and generous and we always enjoyed their company. I didn't know Bill, who left for America in 1927, or Delia who died at age nineteen.

UNCLE JOHNNY

Johnny was the 'character' uncle. He had worked for years in the post office, in Kells. He was into greyhounds quite successfully, being the winner of the first race in Celtic Park, Belfast, in 1927 with 'Mutual Friend'. Anyway, he deserted the safe haven of the post office for the uncertainties of dealing in greyhounds. He gambled on them too and generally had a much more stimulating life than before.

Johnny had a great sense of humour, and a natural bent towards mildly outrageous behaviour. He lived in Dublin, and he always had time for his many nephews and nieces, and indeed anyone from Oldcastle. If you wanted an all-Ireland ticket, Johnny Tuite was your man! We enjoyed him, but with a certain amount of trepidation – something outrageous was bound to be said or done. We always contacted him on the rare occasions we went to Dublin.

I remember once, Pat and myself, then teenagers, meeting him at the Pillar in O'Connell Street. We had collar and tie and in our best. The first thing he did was to grab our ties, straighten them and tuck in the knots, brush off invisible debris from our shoulders, all the while admonishing us to tidy ourselves up, to straighten ourselves up! You can imagine our teenage embarrassment in the full view of the population of O'Connell Street. He took us then to the Green Rooster restaurant nearby and fed us with food and fun.

On another occasion, when I was nine or ten, I was in Dublin with Dad and he left me with Johnny for a while. Johnny was on his way to meet some cronies and he took me along. After introductions and a few minutes chat, I saw Johnny nudging one of them, indicating me and saying "Good lad, Peter" followed by another nudge. The penny dropped and each of them slipped me a half crown. Now, there were two ice-cream parlours in O'Connell Street...!

My brother Pat tells the story about the time Johnny visited him in Limerick, where Pat was working. Johnny was great for keeping in touch. There used to be greyhound auctions in Limerick Junction which he attended regularly. Anyway, they were walking up some street in Limerick after a meal, when they approached a church into which a stream of women was passing. "Come on, let's go in here", he said, and wheeled into the church. Limerick was always a great place for sodalities, and this was one of them. The church was nearly full of women, who were sitting quietly waiting for the service to start. Up the centre marches Johnny, with Pat sheepishly following. As they passed each bench, the women started whispering to each other. Johnny, aware of this, turned around abruptly at the front and said in a loud voice, "Do you hear them now? YAP, YAP, **YAP**"! Pat bolted for the side door!

One day Johnny, Uncle Pee, Eddie's wife Mary and I were coming from the Spring Show in Pee's car. Johnny was anxious to get to the greyhound stadium, and he was directing the reluctant Pee as to how he should get there. That was fun in itself "Follow that car! Turn left – no right here! Get the fleck out of the way! Go home and shave you hairy bugger! Oh God a woman driver, get behind that truck..."! Coming up the quays, we were behind the same truck in slow-moving traffic. The truck stopped and remained stationary. Johnny was getting agitated and after a couple of minutes he jumped out of the car exclaiming "Jazis he's stuck". He stood out in the middle of the other lane, just avoiding being run over to the accompaniment of curses and gesticulations, stopped the traffic and proceeded, with outrageous confidence, swearing and bantering, to extricate Pee from behind the truck. Mary and I enjoyed that

When I took the boat for England on a cold, wet, windy and miserable January in 1957, it was Johnny who accompanied me to Dun Laoghaire and waved me off. That was my last sight of him, as he died shortly afterwards at the age of fifty-nine. My mother died the following year at age fifty three. My boss in Barclay's Bank was loath to permit me to take time off for her funeral in case I was lying! This was a reflection on him, not me.

UNCLE PACKY

When I lived in the Tanyard as a five or six year old, I used to spend as much time as I could next door in the forge, or in Packy's garage. This was where all the action was. It was also where my aunty Kathleen, (not to be confused with Kathleen Brady, Packy's fiancée) worked at the time. Both of them, as always, were very nice to me, and went to the trouble of humouring me. From that time I always had a special relationship with Packy. At the age of fourteen, when I was about to go to St Finian's boarding school, I called in to say goodbye. Before I left he gave me a lovely wrist watch, the first I ever had.

The forge and Packy's garage next door to the Tanyard

Packy was a well-known, if not famous, motorcycle racer, having once recorded the fastest lap in the Skerries One Hundred, the premier motorcycle race in Ireland at the time. When he would be coming from the Kells direction on a summer evening, we would hear the roar of his Norton racing bike while he was on the far side of the mountain. (We always called the Loughcrew Hills 'The Mountain') As soon as we would hear the bike, I and my siblings would rush out to the road from all directions. To our delight, he occasionally stopped and gave us a little ride.

PACKIE TUITE leading STANLEY WOODS at Tallaght in the "Leinster 200" in 1937.

Packy had a contract with the government to supply fuel for Dublin around the end of the war, and he had a few trucks doing that. He drew turf from Frenchpark in Roscommon. My father also did that, so it must have been 1945 or later because his truck was off the road during the course of the war. Packy also bought standing trees, cut them up, and delivered them to the Phoenix Park. I was driven through the Phoenix Park at that time, and there were huge clamps of turf and timber lining the central road almost from end to end, on both sides. It was a handy storage place for some of the heating requirements of Dublin City which, of course at that time had little or no central heating and no coal.

There were some magnificent beech trees around Loughcrew, and I was one day watching the men at work near the Summerbank Road. Packy had bought some standing trees there. Remember again, that muscle energy was all there was, and crosscut saws and axes were the means. Packy took a major shortcut by dynamiting the trees as they stood. I was standing on the safety of the Summerbank road, watching the dynamite at work. One minute there was this beautiful beech tree (a home for the red squirrels of the time), the next there were huge chunks of timber flying through the air. One large half-bole with a spear-like end came down with such force that it almost disappeared into the earth. Those were the days when almost anyone could buy a stick of dynamite.

Years later, at a time when Packy became aware that I was having financial difficulties, I got a phone call from him: "I'll be in the Ardboyne Hotel this evening at 7pm – can you meet me?" After a cup of tea and a desultory conversation, he removed a fat brown envelope from his pocket, handed it to me and said, "Now, I don't want that back". There was a substantial amount of money in it. What a man!

UNCLE PACKY AND THE SUIT
This is another little story in which Packy figures prominently. In 1944 or 1945, when I was ten or eleven, I was on my way to school one day when Uncle Packy met me on the road. He stopped, said "Get in", and stopped again at our house. "Go in and tell your mother you are coming to Dublin with me". My feet had wings, and I didn't give my mother a chance to check me out. Packy had several business meetings in or around the centre of Dublin, and I have only a vague memory of where we went and what we did prior to lunchtime. I do remember at one stage sitting down on the edge of a pavement with my fingers in my ears because of the unbearable traffic noise!

Towards lunchtime, we made our way to the Clarence Hotel, where Packy had arranged a rendezvous with his fiancée, Kathleen Brady. (When I was five or six I had caught them snogging in his office). The Ballinvalley eyes found the hotel and the staff awesome. Everything was motoring along pleasantly, until I was asked by Packy to take off my overcoat. As soon as it was off, he said, "Put it back on", which I did, only then remembering that I had no arse in my trousers. He said to Kathleen, "Hang on here for a while", to me, "Come on", and I traipsed out after him to a gents' outfitters, Kennedy & McSharry I think, in Westmoreland Street. There I got fitted out with a fantastic suit, herringbone grey, hand-stitched lapels, a perfect fit. The old pants went into the bin. The damage, by the way, was not long-term wear and tear but the result of recent slidings down the mountain.

We returned to the hotel and the waiting Kathleen, who was probably on a lunch break and in trouble with her boss by now. By this stage I was starving, and when food finally arrived I could only stare in dismay at the big plate with a couple of little pieces of food artfully arranged on it. I said, "What? Is that all the potatoes I get?" (Brat!) Packy called the waiter over and said, "This young man is from the country – bring him a bucket of potatoes". I didn't quite get a bucketful, but I ate well and went home satisfied with the day, and impatient to show off my lovely new suit to my mother. My confirmation came up shortly after that, and I felt that I was the best-clad lad in the church.

Packy Tuite

A man of empathy, great generosity, and few words was my uncle Packy.

Uncle Mickey (The Yank)

As children we knew little about The Yank, except that he was in the Merchant Navy during the war and that he lived in the USA. What he did there is a bit vague. I suspect he was in the hospitality/catering business, perhaps on a liner or cruise ship. He visited home every couple of years (he never married), and was a welcome visitor to Ballinvalley, because he didn't have crabs in his pockets, and we all went off clutching our little sixpences and sweets. It was on one of his visits that I learned to read.

Mickey was the only one of the family to visit Detroit, where his brother Bill had emigrated to in 1927. Bill never got home again – never saw his mother or his other siblings again. He had four children, Elizabeth and one of her daughters being the only ones I have met. The survivors and their children are scattered around the USA, mostly in Michigan. Mickey returned to Oldcastle on his retirement, and lived in and tended the lovely gardens in the Tanyard. That was knocked down in later years, and it is now a parking lot attached to the garage which Packy's son John now owns. He ended his days peacefully in a nursing home in Dunshaughlin, making chat and joking to the end.

Tanyard Tuites – Delia, Ned, Johnny, Bill, Lillie & baby Mickey c.1908

UNCLE PEE

When I lived with Granny Tuite in the Tanyard during the early part of the war, Uncle Pee still lived there. My impressions of him are vague, but I know that he used to come in for a while and then rush out again, giving me a pat on the head and directing some jocular comments in my direction. I think he must have got into the cattle dealing at that time. His cousin, Jack Smith, father to the future bishop of Meath, Michael, was a big operator in this field, buying around the country, and exporting via Dublin. Pee later got a Land Commission farm in Boolies with a little new house, and it was there that he and Rita Flynn raised their family.

Pee was always good company and had his own little quirky mannerisms that we often imitated away from him. His wife, Rita, whose own home had been in Ballinvalley, was a lovely woman, with a warm interest in people. My father saw some humour in the extent of her interest. Invariably, when Pat and I returned from a visit there, we would be met with, "Well, what did she ask you?" The answer was always, untruthfully, "Nothing". "So what did you tell her?" "Nothing".

Rita's brother Joe was a good friend of mine. A little anecdote about Joe is worth recalling. Apparently Joe, my brother Olo and some local lads used to play cards in Mollsheen's (Molly Galligan's) at Boolies Bridge. Molly had an infestation of warts on one of her hands and she had been pestering Joe to get some water from Gilsenan's 'wart well' next door to him. Joe kept forgetting and one dark evening he decided that he could not disappoint her yet again. He pocketed a 'Baby Power' bottle and stopped off at the bridge to fill it with Inny water. Molly was delighted and applied some immediately to her warts. It is unclear whether Molly's warts were vanquished by the contents of the 'Baby Power' bottle, but it transpired that within a few weeks one of Joe's hands was covered with warts!

Pee and Rita lived a little over two kilometres from us, and their children visited our house frequently. We also spent a lot of time visiting Boolies, and getting to know their neighbours. All my siblings and even my own children have very warm memories of Rita and Pee.

THE AUNTS

Lillie and Kathleen were the aunts, and in a man's world they didn't get as much attention as they deserved. Lillie was gone from Oldcastle before I was born, so I only got to know her when I was 10 or 12. She was married to John Brady, an inspector in the Department of Agriculture, and I suppose we country folk in Ballinvalley felt that she had moved to a different level with her house in Clontarf and all! She was a lovely woman, who had me on a couple of short holidays with them. Her elder son, John, who later became a Jesuit priest, was around my age, and I used to go swimming with him at the Bull Wall. We kept in regular contact over the years. His younger brother Luke became a doctor, and is still practising. Lillie, like Packy, Pee and Mickey, lived into her 90s.

Aunty Kathleen spent some years working in the Irish Hospital Sweepstakes' offices, but most of her life was in Oldcastle or out in Baltrasna, in the Kearney homestead. She did office work for Packy, and spent quite a few years looking after her mother, Granny Tuite, before she died. She was a lovely singer, and she performed on Raidió Éireann occasionally. Most of my siblings were not singers and I remember once when a group of us were in the Tanyard, Kathleen made a fruitless attempt to teach us to sing 'The Mountains of Mourne'. She was married to Donal Kearney, a local solicitor, who, when he was a judge, famously found Charlie Haughey innocent in the Arms Trial. Kathleen loved to welcome us when we visited, and she had a keen interest in our lives and careers and our children. She was pre-deceased by Donal, and lived to a great age. Their only child, John, lives in Toronto.

SIBLINGS

The eleven of us were: Eddie (born 1927), Olo, Michael, Dilly, Pat, myself, Maeve, Marie, Cella, Willie, and Andrew (born 1944).

The Ballinvalley Tuites: Eddie (inset), Olo, Marie, Maeve, Pat, Maggie, Michael & bride, Anne McHugh, Peter, Ned, Dilly, Cella, Willie, Andrew 1954

Eddie went to live in the Tanyard and work in the garage with Uncle Packy when he was 14. He later went to Australia and spent his career in oil exploration in various parts of the world. Olo stayed at home and took over the farm. At the age of seventeen, Michael went off to London, where he got a job in Claridge's. Dilly went to England at 17; Pat left for a job in Navan when he was 14, later moving to New York; Maeve went to London and later to New York; Marie went to London; Cella went to London and from there to New York; and Willie and Andrew also emigrated to London.

My memory of my interaction with my siblings during national school years is pretty cloudy except where Olo and Pat are concerned. Olo, of course, as the farmer designate, was always there and he joined in a lot of our activities, including hunting rabbits and sometimes going walkabout with us younger ones. The main point of contact was when working on the farm or around the farmyard – he was the benign boss. One autumn day he and I went to Soden's field picking mushrooms. On the way back on the bike, with me on the crossbar clinging to the traithníns on which the mushrooms were impaled, my big toe got caught in the front wheel spokes and Olo went over the handlebars. Miraculously, my toe wasn't truncated and the mushrooms survived. Olo had a few scrapes for himself – and a few words for me!

In the main we were a happy gregarious group. Of course we squabbled and sulked, we envied each other and were proud of each other, and if we resorted to violence against each other it was never more than 'hand bagging'. I had seen neighbouring children resort to fisticuffs with their brothers; we did not have to be told that such behaviour would not be tolerated in our family, and indeed we never felt like crossing that line.

Peter, Ned, Marie, Willie, Cella, Andrew - Virginia 1950

Dilly, Michael, Olo and Eddie Tuite 1934

Andrew, Dilly, Peter, Eddie, Willie, Maeve c.1951

Maeve, Pat, friend, Cella, Dad, Dilly, Willie, Andrew, Marie c.1950

COUSINS

Most of my cousins were much younger than me, and I would have seen them only when I would be home on holidays. They would most likely have played with Cella, Willie and Andrew. Of course I called frequently on Packy's and Pee's families as a teenager and in adulthood, and got to know their young children well. They were all lovely children and I enjoyed meeting them. William, Pee's eldest, joined me as a member of the Oldcastle Senior Team later on. Packy's daughter Sheila, then a student, did Trojan work for us in the 1970s in helping us to run a major soft fruit farm in Cork during picking season. John Brady was the only one of my Irish cousins near me in age, but of course we met only very occasionally as he lived in Clontarf. I did enjoy his company when I visited a couple of times on holiday.

Our cousins on my Mother's side lived in Dublin. The young McEvoys, children of my Aunt Sue, used to visit us in Ballinvalley fairly often, particularly Derry, who really loved to come down and lark about in the hay barn and out in the fields. Mam's other sister Bea was estranged and we never met her or her children. Their home was somewhere around Kilbarrack in Dublin.

We were hardly aware of our American cousins, children of my uncle Bill Tuite, as there never seemed to be any communication from Detroit. I have met only one of them, Elizabeth, who was born in Ireland and went to America as a baby. We've been friends for years.

GRANNIES

Mam's mother, Granny Fitzgibbon (née Twamley) was a Protestant, who was written off by her family for marrying a Catholic. I believe that she may never have spoken to or met any of her family again. This kind of stuff happened on both sides then, and for many years afterwards. The husband, our grandfather John Fitzgibbon, was in the British army, based in the early 1900s in Birr, which was a big garrison town, like Oldcastle. He died before I was born, as did Granddad Tuite. He appears to have served in India and Africa. In the 1911 census, the family was recorded as 'Gibbons', not Fitzgibbon, for reasons that are not yet explained. 'John Gibbons' was then recorded as a 'general labourer'. From later research it appears that he may have left the army and re-enlisted around 1914.

We visited our Granny Fitzgibbon only about twice a year so we did not know her too well. Like all Grannies, she had a huge interest in her Grandchildren. We always came away from the visits reluctantly. She lived in a little cottage with her husband Sam Willoughby (our grandfather had died in 1932) in Lisryan, Coole, between Granard, the headquarters of the Norman Tuites, and Castlepollard. Close by were parishes or townlands called Streete and Maine. We used to get fun from repeating a little statement we heard on one of our visits. It went: "The Maine priest married the Coole boy to the Streete girl". I don't remember Granny

Fitzgibbon ever visiting us in Ballinvalley. There was, of course, no transport. She died in the late forties.

Granny Tuite (née Hayden) was an important part of our lives when we were very small. During our national school years we all, seven or eight of us, descended on Granny every weekday for lunch, when I am sure she uttered many wise words to us. She was a keen gardener and her garden was so interesting and beautiful that passersby used to stop to admire it. Right up to her death Granny showed a keen interest in all our doings. I always felt that she took a special interest in me because she mothered me as a five or six year old. She lingered on into her nineties and Aunt Kathleen had a full time job looking after her in her last years.

Granny Tuite (Bridget Hayden) in her Tanyard garden

The Tanyard, Cavan Street, Oldcastle

THE MOTHERLESS MONTHS WITH GRANNY TUITE

When I was about six I lost my mother to hospital, and spent months living with Granny Tuite in the Tanyard. She was a disciplinarian – arising, I suppose, from her husband's early death leaving her with nine young children to rear on her own. She looked after me well but Mam's love was missed with a miserable intensity.

THE NO-NONSENSE MIDWIFE

The Tanyard was a large two-storey house at the lower end of Cavan Street, not more than two hundred metres from the site of the old castle, built by the Plunketts in their heyday. The older Tuite castle which gave Oldcastle its name had been located off the Millbrook Road, just outside the town.

The church is at the other end of town on the Ballinvalley road, probably about a half a mile away. On Sundays Granny had a ritual for seeing me off to Mass: I would be like a greyhound on the leash in my anxiety to get away. Granny made me stand at the door at about fifteen minutes to Mass time. Exactly five minutes later she uttered instructions: "Go straight to the church. Don't delay, don't stop or talk to anyone. When you get there, go straight up to the front seat and sit quietly waiting for the priest. Do not turn around or speak in the church. Come straight home after mass when you have finished seeing your Dad and your brothers and sisters".

The first Sunday I followed orders perfectly with one exception: there was no way that I could sit quietly. I was messing with one or two other children when suddenly *wham*, I got a ferocious slap on the ear from behind. I snapped around to identify the enemy that I was going to do terrible things to: there was the formidable Miss Gibney, the midwife who delivered me. She was looking coolly at me and hissed: "Don't you ever misbehave in church again, Peter Tuite". Do you know, I never did. Any woman who can grab you by the ankles out of the womb and swing you around like a hammer thrower, just to give you a good start in life, deserves the utmost respect! (That is according to my Mother).

THE LITTLE MITCHER

One morning when Granny, unusually, was not on the ball, I was late for school. When I got there I heard my classmates at their prayers, meaning class was already in progress. I was afraid to go in so I headed back up the town, with the intention, I think, of going straight back to Granny. A few hundred yards on and with time for reflection I came to the decision that it might be a good idea to delay going there until lunch time, when my siblings would be there. For the following hours until lunchtime I explored Oldcastle, and had extended visits to a variety of people at their work. I called in to see a man whose name I cannot now recall who had a piggery off Church Street, about opposite Sam & Georgie Lowndes' cobblers' workshop. The pig man was feeding his pigs and I offered my vast experience from my Ballinvalley days to give him a hand! He declined but we had a good chat and he seemed to find my prattling about taking the sow to the boar rather amusing.

When I had worn out my welcome there I crossed the street to visit Sam and Georgie. These middle-aged, young-at-heart brothers were always so warmly welcoming that it was seldom they had no visitors. It was the most popular meeting place for many of the teenage boys and girls around the town. On this occasion I had them to myself and there was much jocular laughter. I must have been an innocent little chatterbox to have caused such merriment. They, of course, would egg me on and I am sure that I played up to them. They were Protestants. When I was a bit older I learned that Sam had an unhappy romance in his younger days. He fell in love with a local girl, a Catholic. They became engaged. This was a signal for some clergy to take a hand and the romance ended. I am not aware whether it was the girl who was intimidated, or Sam, but it was certain that the Catholic community did not like the clerical interference any more than the Protestants did. We, the Ballinvalley Tuites, owe a debt of gratitude to Sam because it was he who introduced Dad to Mam. Apparently he took the trouble to take Dad walking on the road out to Rotheram's, knowing that they would meet Mam on her bicycle doing some routine messages for Mrs Rotheram.

From the cobblers', as I wended my way reluctantly towards the Tanyard, I spotted Sean (pronounced Shan) Kellett and his son Jack in their harness-making shop. In I went, curious about what they were doing and confident that I would be welcomed and could ask them lots of questions about their craft. Sean was stuffing a hames with sisal or some other fibre and Jack was doing the same with a saddle. They got loads of information out of me! From these beginnings the Kelletts moved into mattress making, a business which has not only survived for around seventy years but which has grown into a very successful mattress and bed making enterprise now run by Jack's son Thomas. Anyway, we had a chat as prolonged as I could manage in order to use up more time. By the time that it became clear that I should move on, it was not yet time to join my siblings for lunch, so I made my way down to the railway station by the back way.

Jottings of a Country Boy

The Tanyard was opposite the gates to the station and I could not risk going that way for fear of Granny spotting me. There was nobody about the station, so I entered a carriage and started to play an imaginary game of travel and derring-do. Soon I dozed off and I could have ended up in Drogheda, or even Dublin. Luckily, the carriage was still stationary when I woke up. Panic stricken, as I had no idea how long I had slept, I leapt out of the carriage and legged it towards the station entrance gate. From there I surveyed Cavan Street, then the Tanyard, for signs of my siblings, but they were not to be seen. There was nothing for it but to chance my arm and enter the house as if I were coming from school.

Fortunately they had just arrived and no comment was made at that point. Just as we were about to head off again my brother Pat muttered something about me not being at school, but Granny did not react. She was a bit deaf and I reckoned I was safe from discovery. On the way back to school I loitered behind my siblings and at the first opportunity I slipped into a side street and I was on my own again. After hanging around there for a while I resumed my tour of the town. A couple of rounds of the square and a bit of window shopping later, I got bored with it and decided that a safe haven for me until school was finished was with Matt Gaffney, the farrier. He knew, or knew of, practically everybody around the parish, either through direct contact or, because of his natural curiosity. I was able to update his knowledge about Ballinvalley people even though I was very young. On this visit I brought previous information further up to date. He encouraged me and laughed a lot at my little stories.

This pleasant interlude was rudely interrupted by the sight of Granny coming up the avenue swishing a stick. I could only conclude that her hearing was much better than I thought, or she had let on, and I dashed behind the door. It was a large double door which opened inward. Fully concealed there, I felt that there was a chance that she would not find me. It was all in vain, for she had been following my progress, I think with Lily Markham's help. Lily was a long time maid-cum-general helper and it transpired that Granny, alerted by Pat's comment, had sent Lily to shadow me. I was, of course, scared when Granny peered into my hiding place, and I fully expected to get a good tanning. I cannot remember what she said to me but, coupled with how uneasy I felt looking over my shoulder all day, it was effective. I decided that I would give mitching a miss for the rest of my life. She did not use the stick.

ROMANCE IN THE GARAGE

In my time with Granny I was in and out to the garage when Aunty Kathleen worked there. Occasional suitors would also be in and out. She would have been about twenty eight or nine then. To me she was just my Aunt, but to a lot of the free young men around the town she was an irresistible attraction. One fellow in particular was very persistent. Even though, on the face of it, he appeared to be a pleasant young man, I took a dislike to him, and in the time that I was there I made a point of highlighting to Kathleen all his perceived bad qualities. This had the required effect. Before I returned to my family in Ballinvalley I was delighted to hear Kathleen give him the bum's rush. Her successful suitor, solicitor Donal Kearney, was much more acceptable to me – he played football for Meath!

The garage office seemed to be a place of trysts, as I caught Uncle Packy snogging with Kathleen Brady, his then girlfriend and future wife. I got sixpence to make myself scarce! The same Kathleen was to witness 'the arse out of the trousers' incident in the Clarence several years later.

GILSON ENDOWED SCHOOL, EARLY 1940S. Back Row: Jim Garry, Tom Lynch, Tim Flanagan, Pat Tuite, Johnny McCann, Paddy Walsh, T Foley, Enda Gibney, Jim Lynch, Christy Purcell, Paddy Sheridan, Dessie Crean, Paddy Smith. Middle: Noel Sheridan, Ernie Crean, S. McNamee, John Joe Lynch, S. McDonagh, Michael Mullen, B. Heaney, John Hanley, C. Reilly, J. McCusker, Paddy Burns. Front Row: P. Masterson, P. Daly, Mattie Monaghan, Paddy McCann, P. Breslin, Georgie Griffin, Peter Tuite, Johnny Gavin, Joey Herbstreit, Carl Gibney, a Callan, Peter Tully. Should also include Patsy Bardon, Hal Porter, Patrick Sheridan and Tommy Monaghan. Thanks to Peter Galligan and Eddie Reilly

TEACHERS

MRS LYDON

My first teacher, in Junior Infants, was Mrs Lydon. She was a lovely, motherly woman with whom we all felt secure. She herself was childless but she had an adopted daughter, Eileen Brennan who qualified as a solicitor later and set up a practice in Oldcastle.

Mrs Lydon's classes were mostly 'playschool' activities such as making horses and carts and a variety of animals from corks and matches. The cutting out of body shapes and wheels was a potentially dangerous activity for infants and I was the only pupil allowed to do it. I have no memory of feeling very important or special because of this responsibility. I do know that from an early age we country boys felt that we were physically superior to the 'townies' because of our more active life style. Apart from physically demanding work on the farm (we were encouraged to contribute from an early age) we also had the advantage, in terms of fitness and long term health, of walking to school every day. Our home was two miles from the school and for eight or nine years we walked this four mile round trip every school day. Even on my first day at school I walked it, accompanied by some of my siblings. There was no tearful mother leaving a scared little boy at the door. Mother was too busy dealing with two babies and I was looking forward to the adventure.

MRS LYNCH

Whereas Mrs Lydon was relaxed and smiling, Mrs Lynch, our Senior Infants teacher, was tense and had an appearance of severity. She was really quite nice but it took us some time to adjust to her ways. Initially we were not therefore as happy and relaxed ourselves as we had been with Mrs Lydon. Perhaps the fact that she had to conduct two classes simultaneously in the one room contributed to her tension and mild impatience.

We had two-person desks, but for Irish classes we sat on a long bench with our little knees exposed to Mrs Lynch's bamboo cane. While we chanted

"A-G-U-S, agus", (=and) the cane would be dragged across our knees, much as one would do on a railing. It was not very painful physically but the unfairness of it hurt.

I had an inflating/deflating experience with her once. She called me up, handed me some money and said "Go up to Gibney's shop and buy a new cane for me. Make sure that you choose a really good one". I trotted off happily up the town, stopping here and there to greet and chat to shopkeepers and anyone not in a rush (everyone). I arrived in Gibney's shop and entered into negotiations for the cane. In those days nobody paid the first asking price. After some good-humoured haggling we agreed a price which left both of us feeling the winner. I must have been an awful little brat at age six! I made my leisurely way back to the classroom, swishing the cane on the way.

It turned out that I was too cocky, as Mrs Lynch flummoxed me by asking me "Cé mhéid?" (How much?) Before I could gather my wits about me and convert to Gaelic mode for the answer, she had delivered a slap to each hand with the new best cane, with an admonition to "pay attention next time". It served me right, as when I entered the classroom with the cane I was directing big grins towards my classmates as if to say "Now you're for it"! While Mrs Lynch would be conducting lessons with first class, we in Senior Infants would be listening in. I was able to keep up with First Class and I was usually able to answer a question if no one in First knew it.

One day Mrs Lynch had left the class for a few minutes and I was acting the 'mickey' as usual. As I passed Margaret Hanly's desk, I bent over her for an attempted kiss. At that very moment Mrs Lynch re-entered the room and in her sharpest voice said "Margaret Hanly, what was Peter Tuite doing to you?" With great presence of mind Margaret answered "Please Ma'am, he was trying to bite my nose". I got my two slaps from the best bamboo cane in Oldcastle! Margaret went on to join a contemplative order of nuns. I pray that my mucking about was not the cause of that!

CHARLIE DOUGLAS

Our school in Oldcastle was an endowed school, presumably with endowment conditions. It may be that for that reason we had not one, not two, but three Protestant teachers. Mrs Harford was the headmistress of the secondary school and her husband taught carpentry to the national school fifth and sixth classes. I always enjoyed his classes. Then there was Mr Douglas from somewhere in The Six Counties called Ballymena! We were only about twenty five miles from the border but we might as well have been a thousand, as we never crossed it into that forbidden land of colonisers and colonised, of dark deeds and unfair practices. Mr Douglas took Second Class (I think that I skipped First Class). He was a lovely man who knew how to have his pupils eating out of his hands. He was a keen gardener. When the time for staking the peas was upon us he would ask the class to bring in branches on the way to school for that purpose. The next morning there would be ant-like files of little bodies carrying large branches on all the approaches to the town. My contribution once was half the branches of a young copper beech in the graveyard. Recently, at my brother Olo's funeral, I saw it standing tall and healthy, seventy years after I almost destroyed it.

Charlie had an amusing and effective trick for ensuring that his boys paid attention. If he noticed a boy messing or otherwise not paying attention as he was writing something on the blackboard, he would add a little bird (it normally looked like a seagull) at a corner. "Well Tommy, what was the last thing I wrote on the board"? "The word 'attention' Sir". "Well now Tommy, what about this little birdie here?" "I didn't see that Sir". "Tommy, you were quite correct in recognising the word 'attention'. If you had been paying attention you would have seen me drawing this little bird. What's more, you would have been learning something". The tittering of the rest of the class was deemed to be sufficient punishment for the errant Tommy!

Charlie always had sections of peeled apples in the classroom which he would select and eat throughout the day. Being health conscious, he took long walks on the country roads. On one of his excursions out towards

Ballinvalley he caught me and a couple of my pals fishing for trout in the river Inny. We were in the river at the Boolies Bridge seeking out trout under the stones when we were startled by the well-known voice saying "What are you boys doing there?" I responded: "We're catching trout Sir". "Don't you know that it is illegal to poach for trout?" "Yes we do Sir. Well Sir, we are not very successful at it. We don't think Sergeant Reynolds is going to be bothered with us". "All right boys, enjoy yourselves". Was he chuckling as he walked away?

When Charlie wanted to leave the classroom for a little while he used to give me the pointer and put me in charge of the class in his absence. I did not take that very seriously and just messed about with the lads. Ah, the flaws in my character! It looks as if I may have been a leader who did not want to lead. Later on, in my first year in boarding school I was offered the captaincy of a football team by the President himself but I said "No thanks Father". I guess that this had something to do with being the middle child in a large family. The older brothers took the leadership roles and the younger were content to follow. We enjoyed all the benefits without any of the responsibilities.

DES BOYLAN

Des was another lovely man. He inspired us to an interest in learning with an understated manner and language that concealed a passionate interest in the boys' advancement. He was the one who told us the story of Johnny and Jesus: *Johnny used to visit the church every day. He would rush in, say, "Jesus, this is Johnny", and run off again. On his death bed Johnny heard a voice saying "Johnny, this is Jesus".* Who then would carry on where Johnny left off? Anyway, sure I passed the church on my way to school! Anyway again, if I had not been doing that I would never have seen my Uncle Pee and Rita Flynn getting married. It was a complete surprise to see them at the altar. Communications in large families did not reach very far down the line then. Rita wore a smart red costume and there were only two witnesses visible although I have seen a wedding photograph with the happy couple surrounded by his siblings, his mother and my mam. Hard times and an economic wedding!

Des was manager of the juvenile football team. I had very seldom kicked more than a pig's bladder in the yard at home but I was on the team for a match in Kells despite my young age. I was like a headless chicken during the game, getting only one kick at the ball, and that a panic-stricken boot over the end line for a fifty. After the match the good, kind man congratulated me for my action in saving a certain goal!

We had travelled to Kells by train. When we arrived at the station in good time for the return journey there was a report that the train was delayed. Patsy McEnroe and I decided we would have time to go up town for an ice cream. Our enjoyment of the ice creams on the way back was rudely interrupted by the sight of the train pulling out of the station, windows full of laughing faces. We were twelve miles from home, with no money and no knowledge of how to get there. I asked Patsy if he knew the way, he couldn't be sure. He did have an aunt somewhere in the area but he didn't know exactly where.

My dormant leadership qualities began to awaken and I said "Right, we don't know the way by road so there is only one thing to do: hit the rail line. It goes straight to Oldcastle so we can't go wrong." So off we went, stepping primly on the closely spaced sleepers. We were not to know it but that decision had broad repercussions. We had removed ourselves from hope of rescue, we had created huge worry for Des Boylan and for our families and we had committed ourselves to a long walk of small steps with no hope of a lift. Good decision, leader!

After walking for a couple of hours we were very tired and we lay down for a short rest. It was a balmy April evening. I think that I must have dozed because the next thing I hear is Patsy's plaintive voice saying "Peter, I want to go home". So off we trudged again, the sleeper spacing seeming now more in tune with our tired little legs.

We finally reached the Boolies (railway) Bridge where I took to the road while Patsy continued on to the next bridge from which he cut across the fields to his home. I still had a mile and a half to go, but a half mile from home my father's truck pulled up with a haggard looking Des Boylan in the passenger seat. My father contented himself with asking "Where in the name of God were you?" – not expecting an answer just then – while Des confined himself to asking if Patsy was all right. They had, of course, spent hours searching the roads for us. It was then one o'clock in the morning. Hours of increasingly anxious searching were instantly forgotten. Whew!

When I arrived into the classroom the next morning I was greeted by Des "Here he is, Paul Revere". My travelling companion, Patsy, very sensibly, remained in bed. The following week's edition of the Meath Chronicle had an epic poem entitled "The Night I Walked from Kells".

MR CUMMINS

Mr Cummins was a good teacher with an occasional short fuse. It was in his class that I got a 'crucifixion' injury in my hand. I was messing with and annoying a classmate in the desk in front of me. Suddenly, he lost it, turned around and plunged his nib pen into my hand, right through to the desktop.

Anyway, one of the most memorable incidents occurred in his time: 'The Case of the Missing Button'. One of Georgie Griffin's brothers was messing and Mr Cummins took him to task. Griffin's reaction was not compliant. Mr Cummins got a bit agitated. Verbal hostilities ensued during the course of which Griffin was told to button up his shirt. "I have no button". "Well, go home and get your mother to sew one on". Griffin stamped out the door, closing it with a bang. Ten seconds later he reopened it, stuck his head in, yelled "Fuck you and your button!" and made a run for it. Mr Cummins charged after him, knocking a couple of desks aside on his way – it was like a cop chase. He disappeared out the door after him. We knew that he was not going to catch Griffin. It was now our turn to worry as he would undoubtedly return to class in a vile mood. We were studying Goldsmith at the time and a couple of lines came to mind. (I could recite 'The Deserted Village' from first line to last at that time):

Well had the boding tremblers learned to trace
The day's disasters in his morning face

Mr Cummins may have had the occasional 'flash' but all in all he was an admirable teacher, respected by most of his pupils.

F You 'n' Yer Button by Ailbhe Reilly-Tuite (14)

Georgie Griffin came to my aid on one occasion in the school yard. I had made the mistake of inviting John Hanly to a fight, not knowing that for the previous two years he had been having boxing lessons. Technique overcame brute force and Georgie intervened, warning Hanly to back off or he, Georgie, would skelp him! Georgie was only a little fellow but he was usually able to overcome bigger lads with ferocity. In the nineteen eighties he built our house in Dunshaughlin and made a perfect job of it. Sadly, he died in January 2014.

As an aside, perhaps as a reflection on the rigid attitudes of the time, I was banished from singing classes with one or two others because I 'couldn't sing'. We were herded into an empty room, given poetry books and instructed to learn the poems off by heart while the singing class was in progress. I learned to love 'The Deserted Village' then. Much of it was very relevant to Ireland of the 1940s. Though the country was being denuded of its young men and women, (how history repeats itself), we youngsters were perfectly happy with our quality of life. That is not to say that we did not have some awareness of the dire situation.

But now the sounds of population fail,
No cheerful murmurs fluctuate in the gale,
No busy steps the grass grown foot-way tread,
For all the bloomy flush of life is fled

FRANK SHEEHY

All through national school, I was blessed with good teachers, some perhaps more sensitive and discerning than others. Mr Sheehy was the crowning glory of the group. He came to the school for virtually all of my final year, and from the first day he made a lasting impression on me. He introduced himself something like this:

Boys, people say that I am a good teacher, and I believe I am. My primary task is to enable each of you to fulfil your potential, and I will do everything in my power to achieve this. However, I shall fail if you do not fulfil your part. First of all, you must want, and want passionately, to learn. Secondly, you must apply yourselves diligently to classroom activities and to homework. Anyone in this class who does not want to learn, who is here only because he has no choice about the matter, creates a huge problem for him and for me. I cannot teach someone who does not want to learn. I can teach only those who do.

What choices does the non-learner have? His only choice seems to me to be that he thinks deeply about what life is all about, about the advantages an educated person has over the uneducated, about the lack of choices he will have as an uneducated person. If he is thinking right, he will decide that however difficult it is, he will sit up in class and try his best. If I know he is trying I will give special help. If he is not trying, I am obliged to focus on those who are. Please, anyone who does not intend to try, please go off somewhere – the Hag's Chair on Sliabh na Callaigh, the church, a boat on Lough Sheelin – and think hard about this. It is a once-only chance for you yourself to take control of your life at a critical time.

For those who want to learn, please be confident that I will be able and willing to lead you as far as you are capable of going. As signal of goodwill and intent, I shall arrange later, when we have all settled in, to hold special classes, two mornings weekly at 8.30am. At these we shall study English at an advanced level, and I shall introduce you to geometry and algebra.

He was as good as his word, and about eight of us (out of about thirty) attended those special classes. My problem was that, while I loved the stimulation of classes, I hated homework. A group of us used to have cogging sessions almost every day in Lynch's shed behind their house. As a consequence, much of the benefits of good teaching were diluted without the consolidating effects of homework and study, and the bright young spark that existed up to about class three or four dimmed and almost extinguished.

A memorable event occurred during Mr Sheehy's time. It was winter, one of the hard ones, and Larry Farrelly's pond was frozen solid. Word spread. At lunchtime almost every member of fifth and sixth class hurried down there. Time flew. Mr Sheehy stood at the door of his classroom possibly wondering if he was hallucinating. Where were the children? Not until about a half hour after the allotted time did a trickle of children make their way back, followed ten minutes later by a stampede of boys, only mildly anxious because of the security of numbers. Standing at the door, trying to look angry, Mr Sheehy gave each one of us a token two slaps. The lecture which followed was not token and when we went skating again we made sure that we had someone with us who had a watch.

Frank Sheehy retired some years later, and headed off to Africa as a volunteer teacher. He was outstanding to the end. I believe he died in harness there, teaching those 'who wanted to learn'.

UNNAMED TEACHER

I saw this teacher lashing one of the Reillys from The Terrace *one hundred and ten times*. We had not witnessed any offence. When this teacher took the cane in his hand anything could happen. The cane was a bamboo similar to those which we use to stake flowers in the garden. Because of the regularity of prolonged slapping incidents we had taken to counting the number of hits that he made. In this instance the pupil held out each hand in turn, with the whacked one resting momentarily in his oxter before being again stretched out for the next slap. This went on it seemed forever and not once did the pupil wince or show any emotion. Left hand out, into the oxter; right hand out, into the oxter – in steady rhythm, fifty five in each hand, the savage beating continued. As if the stoicism of the victim was unbearable to the perpetrator, his hits increased in violence until finally, at the one hundred and tenth stroke the teacher wiped his brow, conceded defeat and said "You are an animal." We were lost in admiration for the pupil and disgusted with the teacher. We were also pretty scared. This beating was exceptional but the teacher was consistent in his regular delivery of savage assaults on scared young boys. I was lucky enough to have been in his class only occasionally when he filled in for Mr Cummins. I was even luckier in my timing, as he retired just before I was to move into his class. This teacher also insisted that all those with non-Gaelic surnames such as myself should be identified as foreign by the application of the Irish surname "Ó Geibhigh' instead of their own name.

I was blest with all the teachers who saw me through national school and made it a happy experience. I really did love school in large part because of them. I did mitch twice; once as a six year old and once as a ten year old but neither was related to problems with a teacher.

NEIGHBOURS

Our nearest neighbours were the Bardons on the main road. We did not have much interaction with them except for the youngest, Tommy, nicknamed 'Coinín'. This sobriquet derived from his cash-generating activities as a catcher of rabbits. No pinch of salt for the Coinín! He had snares all over Sliabh na Callaigh in the forties/fifties, and he had regular clients for all the rabbits he caught. He was a lovely young lad, with a great sense of humour. I often saw him with a ferret or stoat peeping out of his pocket. He, and all his generation of Bardons, emigrated to the Derby area in England. Not one of them is left in Ireland or at least not around Oldcastle as far as I am aware.

The McCanns were nearby. We played a lot with them. Paddy and Johnny were around the same age as Pat and me, Jerry was a bit younger. Dotie was a little older than me and Marcella a little younger. We used to envy the boys because, according to their own boasting, they could lay their hands on money very easily. It appears that when their Father had had a bit too much to drink (every fair day), he fell asleep in his chair. He was then easy prey, and the boys dipped into his pockets. They were all enthusiastic participants in our dam building and skinny dipping. Mrs McCann was a favourite of ours. Most of the boys died at a rather young age.

Next nearest were the Blaneys, half a mile up the mountain lane that began at our gate and ended at the foot of the mountain about a mile away. I was very fond of Mrs Blaney from a young age. It was she who gave me the annual task of taking the she-goat to the he-goat. This I did for the sixpence, but also because I enjoyed it, as did Mrs Blaney seeing me being dragged out of the yard by the enthusiastic goat! Her husband, Jimmy Blaney was a big, strong, somewhat rough man who could wrestle bullocks and drink with the best. My brother Pat and I, in our wanderings, were always sure of a welcome and some food from Mrs Blaney. Jimmy Junior lives in the home place. Apart from his brother Tommy who lives in the town, all his siblings emigrated to the Derby area and stayed there.

Jottings of a Country Boy

A little farther up the mountain lane were the Boylans. Ned Boylan was one of our footballing/fighting heroes when we were small. Ned and his brother Frank liked their pints. Those days, under the Legislation, if you lived more than three miles from the pub, the licensing laws didn't apply to you. Every time the Boylans were caught in the pub after hours, they claimed that they were outside the three-mile limit.

As a consequence, the police used to walk out from the pub, dragging a measuring chain, and pushing their bicycles for the return journey. We all knew – the guards knew – that Boylan's house was not outside the three mile limit but for some reason they measured each time. As the guards came up the road and passed our house, we would gather to watch, and to do a bit of discreet sniggering. The Boylans were much older than us, so we did not have much interaction with them. Rosie married and moved a few miles away as a young girl. I met her at a recent funeral and she had to introduce herself.

Beyond the Boylans were the Monaghans. The father, 'Fodgie' was tempestuous. He drove his sons hard on the farm, and had them ploughing and carrying out other heavy work when they were too young for it. He used to come to my father to have letters or other papers read for him. He chased me once as a nine year old when I was cheeky to him. He didn't catch me. His second son, Mattie, was my best school friend. We used to walk to and from school together. Pat and I were often in with poor Mrs Monaghan for company and cake. She was a nice put-upon woman, very quiet and a bit withdrawn in a noisy household. Because we had land adjoining theirs – the mountain field – we passed often. There were thirteen Monaghan children.

Almost opposite the Monaghans were the Reillys. The father, Jack, nicknamed 'The Rat' was a good neighbour, and often joined us at harvest for sheaving and stooking the oats and barley. He was fun to work beside, and when he and Pee Farrelly were working alongside each other in the fields it was a constant pantomime. Jack's children were younger than us, and I hardly knew them. We did know later on that one of his daughters married Joe Dolan's drummer!

The cul-de-sac had a branch off to the west. On the corner of this was Kit Simons. Kit was a bachelor who tolerated us about the place. When the cherries were ripe on the tree he allowed us to pick as many as we could eat on the spot and no more. His source of spring water was a huge deep hole in the ground, about five meters in diameter and four or five deep. If we did a bit of work for him it was not always easy to get paid.

Next up the road were the Flynns. Their daughter, Rita, was married to our Uncle Pee, and their son Joe was a family friend. I remember when his mother died, he raced down to us on his bicycle for my mother. The truck was new and had not yet had its crib built, and I have a clear memory of Joe sitting precariously on the chassis as Olo drove it out of the yard. Joe later sold the farm and took the boat to London. I was there at the time, and was able to look after him until he found his bearings. I was best man at his wedding to Nan Farrelly, from Munterconnaught. Joe was Godfather to our daughter Mary.

I had a terrifying experience once when Pat and I, aged around eight and seven, were taking a shortcut through Flynn's fields. There were two sows there, rooting up the sods and grunting bad humouredly. We were fine with that until Pat ran ahead, jumped up on the ditch and started to call the sows "Muck-muck-muck". At this the sows broke into a gallop towards me making menacing snorts and grunts. Having seen sows eat their young, and not thinking myself much bigger than the piglets, I broke into a terrified race towards the safety of the ditch occupied by my mischievous brother. I was in such terror that I thought that my legs were ossified, and all the while the snorts of the monstrous sows seemed to be warming my backside. But my legs were moving despite my feeling of paralysis, and I just made the ditch a breath away from the terrorists. "What did you do that for?" – got no answer, just a roguish laugh!

Later on, sadly, I visited Joe in hospital the day before he died. He could still laugh through his pain (emphysema, from a lifetime of heavy smoking, was killing him.) He knew he was for it! He said to me, "Peter, the best thing you can do for me now is to go out and buy a lump hammer, come back here and give me a good wallop". This he said with a wheezy laugh. I went back home to Ireland that evening, and I missed his funeral. When Joe's sister, Eileen (McCabe) was on her last legs in a nursing home near Virginia, May and I visited her, even though there was some doubt that she would recognise us. She did, just. I saw a nice few exotic bullocks out the window, so I said, "That's a herd of great bullocks out there". "Aye, Peter, but they're not mine". Maybe she wasn't on her last legs at all.

The house beyond Flynn's was inhabited by an elderly couple, the Cahills. I don't remember ever speaking to them. Beyond them was Gilsenans. There was a well in the Gilsenan's mountain field which had a reputation as a curer of warts! The Gilsenans were egglers, and they reared chickens and turkeys. They were a supplementary source of cash for my farming brother, Olo. He worked for years without a wage, depending on a handout from my father to go to a dance or whatever. (He and Joe Flynn used to go off to dances on their bicycles and we often heard stories of them giving girls a lift home on the bicycle crossbar). We had plenty of laying hens, and Olo was able to intercept the eggs, and send Pat or me with them to Gilsenans, where we got a fair price. Neither Pat nor I ever considered 'diverting' eggs for pocket money. It was Olo's hard-earned wages. (The eggler Gilsenans were not related to Olo's future wife Mary Gilsenan from Newcastle). Mention of 'interception' of the eggs reminds me of my bantam which was a treasured possession. This little chicken was a good layer and Pat used to annoy me by collecting her egg before I could get to it. To forestall that I used to stand beside her when she was due to lay and catch the egg as she dropped it. This was possible because she half-stood up just before the egg emerged.

The last house on this branch of the lane was Mrs Purcell's. Sometimes when we would be going up to the Sturracheen we would go that way for a change. This was one of our favourite houses to visit. Mrs Purcell always had time for us, and goodies. Her son, Christy, is now a neighbour of ours in Dunshaughlin.

There were other neighbours elsewhere: Mary and Pee 'The Jap' Farrelly's property mearned (bordered) our 'Mack's' field. I liked Pee a lot. He was pretty robust in his views about life, living, and all establishment figures, from Parish Priest to Taoiseach. He read the 'News of the World', an ultra-liberal choice in those narrow days. He was not afraid to stand out from the crowd on matters of principle. One Sunday, when the Parish Priest was saying things from the pulpit that were better left unsaid, Pee stood up and lodged his objection in a loud voice. He then stomped noisily out of the church. I was very fond of Mary Caffrey, his wife. In the late fifties Pee, like Joe Flynn, sold his farm and emigrated with his family to England. That is a story for another day. Although it may be worth noting here that when we were both in London in nineteen fifty-seven and his daughter Rose was fifteen, Pee suggested that I should 'wait for her '! May Quinn's arrival on the scene put the kybosh on that!

Another favourite was Mrs Reynolds, up the mountain road (the main road going over the mountain into Kells). She was a widow who lived with one of her sons, Dickie. She kept a special jar of some syrupy liquid for us (maybe molasses), one spoonful each visit. I ran into Dickie once with a borrowed bicycle at a time when I was only learning to cycle.

The bike belonged to Mrs Woods from Newcastle. She and Mam were friendly, possibly because they had known each other when Mam was working for the Protestant Rotherams. They had also been neighbours for a while in Newcastle. The Woodses were one of the fairly few Protestant families to integrate properly with the community. (Hal Porter, a classmate and friend in the National school, was another – in my time he was the only Protestant pupil). Mrs Woods met her future husband in her own home, where her parents occasionally entertained British soldiers from the Prisoner of War camp.

Getting back to the bicycle: it was there against the wall, an irresistible temptation to a learner-rider with no bike. So off I went down the Caldergate Hill gaining speed at a frightening pace and losing control. I crashed violently into Dickie Reynolds! He was walking innocently into town with a friend when his whole world turned upside down. The front wheel went between Dickie's legs from behind and flattened him. The air was blue for a while, but I was small, and he took it well, as I would have expected from a son of Mrs Reynolds. A grandson or great grandson of

Jottings of a Country Boy

Mrs Reynolds had a pub in Dunshaughlin which he named 'Catty Ned's' after a ruined sheebeen on Sliabh na Callaigh.

We called occasionally to Gibney's, next door to Reynolds'. The father, a widower, seemed to be always kneeling up on a chair saying the rosary. They had a hedge of gooseberries, which was of interest to us in season. When passing by Gibney's, we always threw a stone at the remaining leaves of a medium-sized sycamore tree near their house. The Gibney boys used this tree for target practice. They would pick out a leaf and throw stones at it until it fell, until, by the end of summer, all the leaves would be gone.

Close to that lived the Sheridans. The name was well known through the fame of Monica Sheridan, a cook on radio and later on television, and her husband, Niall, another public figure. Niall's father was keen to teach me chess at a young age, but I resisted, being too interested in the outdoors.

Down the road a bit lived the Hamiltons. They were family friends for a long time, but that was brought to a premature end over land. They were cottagers who had been given a few acres by the Land Commission, with the proviso that they must work it themselves. They, and another cottager called Mack (not our Paddy Mack), did not observe this stipulation, renting it out instead. The Land Commission took the land off them. Hamilton's field, which adjoined ours, was offered to my father. Out of friendship he refused with great regret, because it would have been a perfect addition.

However, he had no scruples about accepting Mack's field, located on the far side of Hamilton's. Land raises terrible passions in people, and when my father called to the Hamiltons to discuss what he was not and was doing, Mrs Hamilton took a pitchfork to him. Luckily for both of them he managed to evade it. This was very distressing for everybody. I played football with their sons subsequently. I got a lift to school one frosty morning when I was in Mrs Lynch's class on the crossbar of Paddy Hamilton's bike. My hands were in such a state (never having gloves) that when I arrived at the school toilet I had to resort to pissing on them to bring them back to life! Resourceful me!

TOWN

We did not have much to do with the town while we were growing up. Our experience of it was more or less confined to a few visits in the year. If the school had been the far side of the town there would have been more opportunities to get to know it better simply by walking through it on a daily basis.

The Square, Oldcastle © Eric Jones, licensed for reuse – Creative Commons Licence

One of the shopping trips to which I always looked forward on an annual or biennial basis was the visit to Jack Crean's drapery shop at the top of the town to buy a pair of boots. When the current pair of boots wore out or were grown out of, Dad would take the lucky person individually into Crean's to be the centre of attention for a little while, and to observe with great attention the pantomime that buying a pair of boots became!

After a lot of toing-and-froing, a boot would be selected, (It was always the same boot as in previous years except for the size,) and the negotiations would begin on price. Jack would wail about losing money on the deal and Dad would head for the door a couple of times, but eventually a deal would be struck and I would walk out in the new boots straight away. In addition to the boots, I also had a new slant on how big a part half-concealed humour played in the negotiating process, which was only fully acknowledged when farewells were being made. (On another occasion when Dad was buying a hat in Kennedy & McSharry's in Westmoreland Street – the very same shop where Uncle Packy bought me the suit – he walked away and was called back from the door five times, with an amused me in support, before the deal was done).

At the first opportunity, I would call in to Sam and Georgie Lowndes to have the metal studs attached to my new boots. There I would be introduced to other young people, and Sam particularly would soon have us all on friendly terms. Many a teenage romance started there.

On Christmas Eve we all accompanied Dad and sometimes Mam, when she wasn't having babies, into town. We would each get a sixpence or a shilling and be left to our own devices until Mass time. The shops stayed open very late. Much time would be spent window shopping, noses pressed against the glass, and sighing over all the lovely toys we would never have. In the end we would buy sweets and forget about the toys. You could get a big bag of bonbons for sixpence.

We never had a party in our house, although we were aware that our townie classmates did have them regularly. I was at one of these parties once on the invitation of FX O'Reilly, one of my classmates at national school and later on, in St Finian's. I was really embarrassed because there were girls there and the lads were making eejits of themselves in front of them with silly games. I did not enjoy it at all and if I had ever received a similar invitation I would certainly have refused it!

Of course we had to walk through the town to get to Granny's for lunch, but we were always under time pressure and there was no time for socialising with any except the 'Corner Boys'. These were the regulars who stood around the busiest corner and passed the time of day trying to take the pain out of a life without work, without income, and sometimes without hope – but always with humour. Among them was a veteran of the Great War who survived almost intact. He just had a vacant, somewhat haunted look about him at times. His name was Jimmy Daly. Jimmy was not quite as damaged as he sometimes seemed because he had retained a strong sense of humour and liked to play tricks on people. I cannot now remember the detail, but there were many versions of his role in the war, most of them contradictory, but all funny enough to generate guffaws in his listeners.

I have memories of the shops and their owners, many now no longer in existence: Des O'Connell in the Pharmacy in Cavan Street, who sometimes hung about the corner with Jimmy Daly. Then there were the Misses Carroll in the corner shop who sold sweets and newspapers. They would have had many children as regular customers because they knew how to please children.

Leo Herbstreit in the square was the barber, who also sold sweets. A group of men, my father included, used to gather there after closing to play cards. On and off during the evening Leo would reach out and take some money out of the pot on the table to cover his expenses – lighting and the handful of sweets that he threw on the table now and again. I know this detail because I had to hang around sometimes waiting for my father. Leo had two sons, Joe and Johnny; and two daughters, Mamie and Norrie. Joe was my age and a friend. Mamie married Batty McEnroe, a brother of Patsy who walked the railway line from Kells with me. Carroll's drapery was prominent in The Square, as was Tuite's restaurant (these Tuites were not known to be related). When the Black and Tans were rampaging around the town on one occasion they fired into the restaurant and smashed a lot of glass. The establishment buildings – the barracks and the C of I church – were also on the square at opposite ends and they remain unchanged. Gibney's shop, where we sold our wool and where I bought the cane for Mrs Lynch, is still in the Square. It was a hardware-grocery-general merchandise store. Charlie Gibney was the owner then. His son, Jim, has run the business for many years since.

Porter's shop, close to the Church of Ireland, was owned by a family called Chambers. It sold groceries and hardware and did good business over a number of years. Then in the fifties I returned on holidays to discover that the shop was doing very little business, apparently because it had upset its Catholic customers by advertising for Protestant staff. It was later purchased by the Co-Op.

Owen Clarke had a prosperous retail and wholesale grocery business. His son Eamon married Carmel Smith, a second cousin of mine. He was a bit older than me. We played football together for a while with the Oldcastle Senior Team in the fifties. As far as I know the business continues. During my time in St Finian's one of Owen's vans, by arrangement with the parents, called into the college every Saturday with food packages for all the Oldcastle boys. The agreeable Tommy Curran was the van man. Andy Carroll owned The Naper Arms Hotel and I think he had a stake in the cinema with Owen Clark. He also had land outside the town.

Down from Owen Clarke's was Robert Trinnear's hardware shop, where Maeve's future husband, John Furlong, worked. Robert, a Protestant, was an amiable man and he had a good business, as indeed had Porter's shop until the insertion of that advertisement. Trinnear's business failed in time, mostly as I understand it, because Robert's father had gone too easy on his many creditors in the community over a long period. These debts largely turned out to be uncollectible and I suppose there must have been obligations on the books to the local banks. Robert and family moved to Dublin. Roberts's sister Bea went out with Donal Kearney for a number of years before he hitched up to my Aunty Kathleen.

Tommy Ashe had a joinery workshop down beyond the cinema. He was a bit of a character, a little outrageous. I remember a statement he made coming out of Lough Derg, the pilgrimage lake, in 1954 or 1955: "There now, I'm all cleaned out. Another year of sinning ahead!" Tommy, my Dad and some of his cattle dealing pals were in their element in Lough Derg as they could sit around all day chatting.

Mickey Cadden was another grocer, held in high esteem by us young ones because of his boxing prowess. Later on, an ex-classmate of mine, Sean Callan had to pay him five shillings a week for the privilege of working for him as part of an iniquitous apprenticeship system.

Down outside the Catholic Church and not too far from the schools, was Flanagan's sweet shop. You could get a halfpenny worth of sweets there and a tuppenny ice-cream wafer, and plenty of enquiries about this one and that one in your family. Sean Timmons at the age of seven or eight was noted for going into the shop every day at lunchtime with a penny in his little fist. "A fag, a match and a halfpenny worth of NKMs please, Ma'am" was his order, and he got them! NKMs were a toffee sweet, a favourite of the children. When The Yank was home on holidays we would hang around him after Mass until he 'dropped' a thrupenny or sixpenny bit, which was promptly added to Mrs Flanagan's till. Her son, Tim, was a classmate and friend. He emigrated to San Francisco and may never have returned except to bury his parents.

Close by in Church Street lived Tom Tilson. In legal circles the name is familiar to family lawyers. It appears that one of the Tilsons, a Protestant, married a Catholic girl and gave all the usual commitments to bring the children up as Catholics. The mother died and the Tilsons began to raise the children as Protestants. There was legal action resulting in a judgement that they could not renege on the commitments. This judgement established a precedent and became known as 'The Tilson Case'. I used to see and greet Tom Tilson who often stood at his door as we passed by.

Not a hundred yards further on lived two Lynch families: Phil Lynch and his wife, parents of Eithne and Monica; and Lynches the musicians who used to entertain us all with brilliant Irish music when they were only children. They went on, of course, to become one of the best known bands in the midlands and beyond for many years afterwards. Michael the TD was in the class behind me and John Joe and Oliver soldiered with me in the Oldcastle senior team for a few years afterwards. It was in this Lynch's shed that we used to do our cogging every morning.

Further up the street, almost opposite Sam and Georgie's workshop was Sean Geraghty the tailor. Beside him were other Lynches, the Ballroom Lynches – so called because they owned the Eldorado Ballroom out towards the graveyard. It was ballroom boom time and the ballroom often had over a thousand dancers on special occasions when included in the ticket price was an entry to a raffle for a new car. Terry, an attractive teenage daughter, used sit on a windowsill outside their house and she seemed to enjoy the attention the boys gave her as they passed by. Hughie, her brother, married another second cousin of mine, Sheila Smith, herself a cousin of Carmel (Smith) Clarke.

A few doors up from Lynches was the Freemason Hall. They got a lovely new building in the sixties at ratepayers' expense after the old one was set alight by two inebriated young fellows.

Then there was Jack Gilsenan's shop. His sisters, Queenie and Dotie lived with him. Jack was a great supporter of the football team. He was an enthusiastic advocate of massage and he was happy to provide free leg massages to members of the team. I was always a disappointment to him as I never sought his services when I was young. He had passed away by the time that I appreciated the value of massage, especially after a hard game.

Down Barrack Street and mearning the Fair Green was the McGinn family. Sean, the son, did well in his career, ending up as CEO of a pharmaceutical company in Dublin. On Cavan Street, close to Des O'Connell's pharmacy, was Smyth's pub. Two brothers owned it, but I think they fell out and one of them went off elsewhere. In later years it was a favourite halting site for the Oldcastle team after a game, as Brendan Smyth was a team member. There were some rows in and around the pub in the early 1950s when Meath and Cavan were top Gaelic football teams and fierce rivals. The Cavan border was only about three kilometres outside the town. A kettle of boiling water was once poured from an upstairs window on Cavan supporters below.

Doctor Hanly, our family doctor lived just beyond the old Prisoner of War camp. His son Michael, who died youngish, was on the St Finian's Gaelic football team with me in 1953, when we won the Leinster championship. Opposite Hanly's was Larry Farrelly's farm. It was here that we enjoyed the pond skating in Frank Sheehy's time. Larry Farrelly was the local milkman who distributed milk in a tin jug to the locals from his cart. None of them died from it!

Back beside Crean's was Mullen's shop, dealing also in clothing, I think, and perhaps furniture. Michael Mullen, who succeeded to the business and who died recently, had a national reputation as an antiques auctioneer. Locally he was held in the highest regard for his contribution to the community over many years.

Going back to St Finian's after Christmas was a miserable experience and a young Mullen, a Crean and an Egginton took extreme measures in their first year to avoid it. They were dropped at the door of the college on a bitterly cold January night and as soon as the car was out of sight they set off walking back to Oldcastle in the wintery darkness. The journey is about thirty kilometres and they made it only to Castlepollard, about half way. There they were settling themselves into a haybarn for the night when the owner found them and took them in. Of course he made all the necessary phone calls and the next morning the boys were dumped back at the college to the amusement of the other hundred and seventy pupils.

Maureen Grace O'Reilly's shop-pub was close to the barracks. It was from O'Reilly's pub that the Guards measured out to Ned Boylan's house, not once, but twice. Maureen, whose son FX was in my class, was responsible for me going to Finian's instead of to the perfectly adequate local Gilson Endowed School. I had, unfortunately, expressed to her an interest in going after the closing time for applications and she arranged a special interview with the school for me. (There were many good things about boarding school, but overall it was a bit of a desert which stunted social development and cut children off from their communities at a critical time in their lives). When I got to the college I was a bit overwhelmed because the interviewers were the outgoing president, Fr Cogan and the incoming President Fr Fagan. Fr Cogan was going off happily to become Parish Priest in Ratoath. They asked me a few questions and gave me a paragraph to read which was grand as I was a good reader. I was disappointed when school started to find that I was in the second, not the first stream.

At the end of the year, my cousin Frank Smith and I were adjudged the top students in the class and we were promoted to the first stream. This progression was all messed up by the effects of the scabies and I was demoted to the second stream the following year, Intermediate Exam year. Luckily enough I recovered lost ground and ended up with nine good honours in the Inter and recognition as the top student of English in the school. The post-Intermediate year was disastrous as I didn't do a tap of work and I wasn't found out because I had flu at end-of-year exams and avoided them altogether. As my father would say: "Well, y'auld eejit,"

HUGH 'THE HOP' DEVINE

The Hop was a class or two ahead of me. He was a heavily muscled, chesty boy with a short leg, hence the nickname. I used to be fascinated looking at him under the cane – I cannot say getting slapped because, despite the teacher's best efforts, he never connected. The Hop's hands and arms were like pistons during the caning process. They would be extended and immediately retracted, at speed. Time and time again the teacher would miss, and in the end send him back to his seat without a mark on him. (This was the cruel teacher who delivered the one hundred and ten slaps to young Reilly).

The Hop was a bit of a character, an enthusiastic supporter of the local GAA team on which his brother Mickey (Micksheen) played alongside me. He had a stentorian voice and in one game when I did something right, this booming voice rose above all other noises to bellow: "Good man young Tuite". I wasn't at all embarrassed! The Hop left school at fourteen and I think he went straight into Sean Kellett's expanding mattress business. The Hop used to travel around to dances. One night he sought admittance to a dance in the Beechmount dancehall in Navan, a venue that considered itself superior to most other dancehalls. He was slightly inebriated and was refused admittance. With some anger and not a little humour, he took a stance alongside the queue and declared: "I've been to dancehalls in Cashelrahan. I've been to dances in Ballinagh. I've been to dancehalls in Mountnugent and Mullaghoran. But this dancehall is the greatest *%!"*! kip of them all"! Needless to say, the rural dancehalls he mentioned might not then have been quite up to the standard of Navan's prestigious hotel ballroom.

JIMMY 'THE DUMP' CAFFREY

Jimmy The Dump, was so called because he had the contract for refuse collection in Oldcastle. I remember seeing him collect around the town with a horse and cart. He was a very affable man, and he was a central character in one of my football experiences. At one time Ballinvalley formed its own GAA football team, a kind of mini-breakaway from the dominant Oldcastle team. We did not have one decent footballer, but we had one or two fierce warriors. In those days every match evolved into a brawl; football pitches really were battlefields. The kids' real heroes were not the best footballers, but the best fighters. Ned Boylan was one of our favourites. About seventy years ago, Ballinvalley were playing in Ballinlough. Jimmy was playing full-back, and I think Barney (?) Coyle was in goal. My favourite viewing position was behind our own goal. There was no fencing in those days. The opposition floated a long high ball in towards the square, and Jimmy shouted to the goalie, "The ball is yours, the man is mine". The on-rushing forward ran into Jimmy's fist, much to my delight, and took no further part in the game.

Five or six years later, Jimmy was the coach to the Oldcastle juvenile team which was being well beaten at half time. He was not pleased with the commitment of the team and to my embarrassment said "Young Tuite there is the only one who is trying". I had been putting a lot of commitment into my play but I would not have been boasting about my effectiveness. In later years, Jimmy built up a successful business, creating good employment in Oldcastle. He had a tragic end, and he would never have guessed at how many like me were deeply saddened by it. His sister Mary was married to our neighbour Pee Farrelly. She was a very gentle, kind woman.

WORK

WARTIME FUEL

During the war there was no coal, and for a time until we got organised, there was little turf. Before we rented the turf bank we would buy a standing tree from someone around Loughcrew. There were plenty of trees in and around the Naper estate. We had our own crosscut saw and axes. The tree would be felled, cut into portable sections and carted home. There we would all have turns on the crosscut to admonitions from Dad to "Pull, don't push". We eventually rented a turf bank in Roebuck, near Mountnugent, from which we were able to harvest a yearly supply.

I have pleasant memories of turf cutting days in Roebuck bog. The turf there was of a high quality, black and dense with long burning qualities. My brothers Olo and Pat and I would normally take on the task supported by the artistry of Paddy 'The Bosheen' Brady. The Bosheen had participated in 'Hiring Fairs' in his young days. These fairs were basically auctions, not of cattle, but of young lads and lassies seeking employment. Contracts would be entered into for three, six or twelve months. The employees would be housed and fed (in the Bosheen's time one bowl of corn or Indian meal a day), and paid the agreed wage, but not until the end of the period. The system was a very small step above slavery!

The Bosheen would be the slanesman, throwing the slippery sods up to us on the bank from below. He was an old man then but he cut and threw sods all day every day with the rhythm of a top golfer. We never wanted work to be too boring, so sometimes we deliberately allowed the sods to fall back down on the Bosheen. His reaction was fairly predictable: for the first one he would just take his hat off, wipe the perspiration from his forehead and give us a cool look. The second time he got contrary and issued dire warnings of a fate worse than death if we dropped another one. The third and last time we were being chased down the bog by a slane-waving lunatic! Bog 'trotters' would not be an accurate description of the participants. We sometimes wondered if he enjoyed the game and if, perhaps, he welcomed the respite from Goldsmith's "unremitting toil". In any event we weren't going to let him catch us just in case, and we made sure that no more sods fell on top of him.

The caught sods were placed on a long flat all wooden wheelbarrow which one of us wheeled away for laying on the ground apart, while the other continued to catch. I can't remember what Olo would be doing but I am sure there was more to it than cutting, catching and wheel-barrowing, although I have a hazy recollection of him sometimes just dropping us off in the cart and returning for us in the evening.

The time we liked most of all was towards noon, when Pat and I were tasked with going to the well for water, lighting a fire and boiling the kettle for tea. This we would do, making sure that we inserted a little piece of stick in the kettle to prevent the tea from being smoky. However, the short walk to the well was very often extended beyond a few minutes by chats with other renters, or exploration of the terrain, or anything that would extend our rest from the turf face, although we never made it to Lough Sheelin a short distance away. The delayed return from the well was not popular with Olo and The Bosheen.

Back to work. The process for saving the turf was simple – a couple of weeks after cutting, when the sods would have lost some of their moisture, we would return to the bog to do what is called 'footing'. This involved lifting the sods from flat on the ground on to their ends in little pyramids so that the air could circulate. Sometimes, after a few weeks, we could transport the turf home and clamp it near the house; other years we might make mini clamps on the bog for several weeks more before storage – a lot depended on the weather. You probably never saw a flea? I don't know whether the annoying little insects are still around, but if they are you will find them in clamps of turf. (This is just in case!)

Before we got the turf every source of energy was tapped. We had stone walls and few trees, so there were not many sources. Coal imports ceased early on in the war. Remember, we had no electricity, gas or running water, and really the only natural source freely available to us was cow patties. Yes, cow patties! When the summer sun dries up the cow patties they become combustible and they generate a reasonable amount of heat (and a strong musky odour). Pat and I seemed to always get the job of collecting these things. We didn't like it, but we managed to make it a fun thing, chasing an old pram over the fields, competing for the best patty, and occasionally throwing them at each other. A pramful would give enough energy to bake a cake, boil a kettle and cook a huge pot of potatoes or porridge.

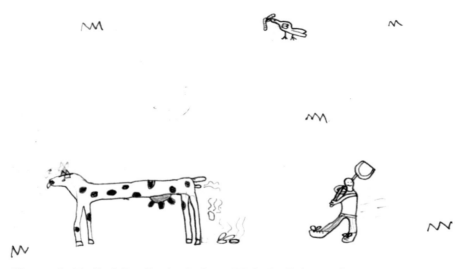

Hot on the Trail of Cow Patties by Isaac Mulcahy Tuite age 8

That was a summer thing – all I can remember of the winter is that I was always cold in the house! Eight or nine of us huddled around the range meant that there was an outside row not getting much heat! (There were seventeen years between the eldest and the youngest so the whole thirteen of us would never be together jostling for a warm spot). On top of that, when wind and rain came at us from an easterly or westerly direction, our lovely, new, Government-built house required buckets in the upstairs bedrooms to aid the shoddy work of the tiled roof!

FARM WORK

Oats and beans and barley grow,
Oats and beans and barley grow,
Do you, or I, or anyone know
How oats and beans and barley grow?

First the farmer sows his seed
Then he stands and takes his ease.
He stamps his foot and claps his hands,
And turns around to view the land.
(Old Nursery Rhyme/Song)

For the benefit of my grandchildren, none of whom are likely to have the privilege of growing up on a farm, I am going to describe in some detail what was involved in farming when I was growing up in the nineteen thirties, forties and fifties. It was not all boring work, and if some of it were, we enlivened it with humour and wit. In Ballinvalley we grew the following crops: Grass; Flax (linen raw material); Grain — Oats, Barley and Wheat; Vegetables — Potatoes, Turnips, Mangold-Wurzels, Sugar Beet, Beetroot, Carrots, Parsnips, Cabbage, Greens; Lettuce, Onions, and Peas in the garden.

PLOUGHING AND HARROWING (GRAIN)

The little nursery rhyme above has got ahead of itself. Sowing the seed is not the first step; the land must be ploughed and harrowed first. Ploughing was a hard physical task. Nowadays, tractors roar out on to fields with, perhaps, ten ploughshares attached at the back and they can plough many acres in a few hours. In the nineteen thirties, forties, and even into the fifties, when your power came from the horse, there might be only one ploughshare, at best two. The ploughman had to walk slowly behind the plough, keeping it upright and steady to ensure that the sod turned over at the correct angle and stayed in position — not an easy task. There was a wheel attached to the front of the plough to maintain a consistent depth. If the plough hit a rock or a large stone the metal handles could inflict a severe injury with a whiplash. If there was only one horse pulling there would invariably be only one ploughshare attached. This would turn one scraw over, not more than four or five inches thick and perhaps ten inches wide. By my calculation, on a perfect run, an acre would take about a day to plough. Rests for the horses and occasional mechanical adjustments are taken into account. With two horses and a second ploughshare attached that time would be almost halved.

Ploughing would have been too demanding for a little fellow like me, but harrowing, the next stage in the process, was a different matter.

Harrowing was the process whereby you broke up the sods, levelling the soil as you went, thus preparing it for the seeds. There was no winter corn in those days; all sowing was in the spring, before April if weather permitted. The harrow was a piece of equipment composed of a number of light beams, maybe ten centimetres square by two hundred and forty long. They were bound together about eight to twelve inches apart. Protruding from each beam would be six-to-eight-inch spikes, eight inches apart. The harrow was pulled by two horses.

I loved harrowing. On a balmy April day my bare feet would be sinking into the soft warm soil as I followed the horses. The now friable clay would be squeezing up between my toes and sometimes I had the feeling that I was anchored to Mother Earth. Seagulls would be in the air and on the ground around us, robins would be arriving out of the blue. The horses and I would be in harmony, aromas from the earth filled the senses. All was right with the world.

The first harrowing done, it was now time to sow the seed. My brother Olo always hand-spread it from a tucked-up apron. Some farmers had a kind of winnowing instrument which blew the seed for a more consistent spread. When Olo would be nearly finished I would follow on again with a harrow to imbed the seeds. Not until then would we all 'stand and take our ease', leaving the rest to nature until harvest time.

We used no sprays or chemicals of any kind on grain. Yields nowadays are considerably higher due to the use of chemicals and the development of seed for winter sowing. Harvesting is much earlier – in recent times I have seen it taking place in July. September was our month to harvest, and what fun it was!

Harvesting Grain

Until after the war when we bought a horse-drawn mower, our entire corn cutting was done by scythe. 'The Bosheen Brady' was acknowledged as the best scythesman around. As he did with the slane, he worked solidly for

hours at a slow but effective rhythm. Some of us would follow him gathering the corn into sheaves, extracting about a dozen straws with which each sheaf would be tied. The tying would be done in such a way that the seeds in the tie band extended up towards the seeds at the top of the sheaf. This allowed the thresher or the winnower to extract the seeds from the dozen straws; otherwise they would be lost to the crows or the geese. The sheaves would be thrown aside and the next person in the work line would build stooks with them. Stooks were built with five or six sheaves standing on their ends and leaning against each other in the shape of a pyramid. These pyramids would be capped by placing one or two sheaves over each one, head-down, as a kind of hat, to let the rain runoff. They would be left to dry-out there for a week or two, after which they would be transferred to the haggard and stacked to await the thresher.

Threshing was a favourite activity for us children. Apart from the fascination of watching sheaves being converted into bags of grain, the now seedless straw thrown out loosely on the ground and the chaff swirling around in the wind, we also had the fun of chasing down all the mice and the occasional rat, as they dashed out of their hiding place in the last sheaves in the stack. The dogs enjoyed this too. Of course all the neighbours would be in attendance, feeding the sheaves into the thresher, bagging and removing the seed, gathering and stacking the straw and generally making themselves useful. There would be lots of banter, especially when the food and drink arrived.

Steam Threshing 1944 by Bob Kavanagh
http://history-links.blogspot.ie/2011/03/day-of-threshing-my-memories-by-bob.html

I missed the threshing one year around the end of the war through misadventure. Pat and I had had a school medical examination and were sent up to Navan Hospital for attention. It appeared that I needed my tonsils removed and Pat needed glasses. However, probably because we have the same initial for our Christian names, there was a mix-up by the school doctor; I got Pat's tonsils out and he got my glasses! He threw them away after a couple of weeks. The aftermath of this unwarranted operation was so severe that I was confined to bed for a number of days, including threshing day. The truth of the matter was that I was as sick about missing the threshing as I was from the surgeon's knife!

The straw would be stored in the barn or built up into another stack and the grain would be stored in a dry outhouse. In due course, when the grain would be needed for domestic or animal food it would be taken to O'Reilly's Mill in Millbrook for refining under the big water-powered grinders.

When we had only scythe cutting, there was little need for outside help because of the slow pace. When we got a horse-drawn mower, quite a few bodies were needed to keep pace with it and we then had help from neighbours, generally Pee Farrelly and Jack Reilly, and perhaps one of the Blaneys. Later on Michael McHugh would take part after he bought Kit Simon's. This help was reciprocated when the neighbours were doing their own harvesting.

Pee, Jack and Jimmy Blaney served up a rich cocktail of witty banter as they slaved away in the heat, and we young ones made sure that we heard every word, including a rich treasury of swearwords. This was only achieved by extraordinary effort. To remain within earshot of them we had to work on the double, stooking their cast-aside sheaves, in order to keep up. We would be tired and happy at the end of the day. My brother Olo had a habit, when asked a question, to preface the answer with "I dunno". On one occasion, as we moved up the field, I heard Jack repeat again and again "I dunno, says Olo Tuite, I dunno says Olo Tuite".

We never tilled a field accessible to the farmyard geese, so our geese never got an opportunity to enjoy feeding in the stubble. Some other farmers' geese were luckier and they got to enjoy Foghmhar na nGéana – Harvest of the Geese.

I must not forget to mention the pleasure of having our midday meal brought out to us in the field. The food would vary from day to day but we always got a can of fresh buttermilk with it and this, embellished by the fresh air, tasted like nectar in our thirsty throats. The girls, who seldom worked outside the house, would deliver the food and stay for some banter before gathering up the utensils and returning to the house. Just for the record, the boys never did housework, except for the drawing of drinking water and the collection of wood or coal for the fire – oh, and turning the churn handle!

During our time in the fields, whether sowing, harvesting or haymaking, a familiar and welcome sound was that of the Angelus bell floating across the fields. It was doubly welcome because it gave an excuse to have a little rest, and for the smokers, a chance to light up. From recurring correspondence in the Irish Times you would think that we would be doing a triumphant jig and chanting sectarian songs! Ah well, some people are easily offended!

VEGETABLES

POTATOES

For the potatoes the earth was ploughed and harrowed as for grain. Two harrowings would be required to get the soil into a fine tilth. To make the drills in which the potatoes would be sown, two ploughshares would be attached to the plough, one to each side. As Olo moved up along the field, two horses pulling, the ploughshares would make half a drill on each side. At the top of the field he would turn around, move in the opposite direction and one ploughshare would complete a drill while the other created another half, and so on he went until all the drills were in place. Of course, at the top of the field he would have to take a wide turn in order to manoeuvre the plough into position for the return journey. He achieved this by starting a new drill further up the headland. He would then go up one drill and down the other to complete his drills.

The next day he would load up the cart with well-rotted manure. He would drive the horse up and down the drills spreading the manure lightly in the hollows. We would follow after with the seed potatoes in aprons, dropping them every thirty centimetres or so. When this was all done he yoked up the horses again to the plough and went up and down the field with the plough in the centre of the drills. The effect of this was that new drills were made over the potatoes and what had been drills would now be hollows.

Nowadays, just about as the potatoes are emerging, the weeds are sprayed with a weed killer which keeps the drills free of weeds until almost digging time. Back then, we allowed the weeds to grow to a height of about 15cm, at which stage they were scuffled.

A Scuffler was a sort of harrow, narrow enough to be pulled between two drills. Instead of spikes it had six flat prongs, semi-circular in shape, a bit like a new moon. These were set up in an iron  frame with handles just like those of a plough in such a way that when dragged along the drill by a horse they ripped up the weeds. One scuffling might be enough but a second would be done if necessary. The scuffling would knock some of the soil off the drills into the hollows so moulding followed. You could have a special mouldboard to do it but Olo used the plough. He simply ran the plough up and down the furrows, rebuilding the soil back on to the drills.

When the flowers were beginning to show on the stalks they were sprayed, then as now, with a special anti-fungicide to prevent blight, (the major cause of the Great Famine.) We used a mixture of 'blue' and washing soda. Today the farmers have machines to dig and sort the potatoes but then we had to do it by hand. This was a very laborious process. Olo and Paddy Mack dug away all day, separating the potatoes from the stalks and levelling the soil as they did it. We little ones would come behind, sorting and picking the potatoes and bagging them ready for storage over the winter. We normally planted Kerr's Pinks for the main crop and a few drills of Golden Wonders. These Golden Wonders were a poorish cropper, but very tasty, and they kept better than any other potato. For a few years we also planted some 'Black Champions'. These were a purplish potato which produced small 'apples' on the stalks. We considered these fruits inedible and harvested only the tubers.

Potatoes do not take kindly to frost and the traditional way to ensure a frost-free environment was to dig a pit about fifty centimetres deep, and tip the potatoes into it until they were fifty centimetres above ground level. We then covered them with a layer of straw fifteen centimetres thick and on top of that we would throw the soil taken out of the pit. It worked well. In the spring we would sort out the seed potatoes, either by choosing smallish ones or by cutting the bigger ones in half, making sure that an emerging stalk was on each, and the whole process would begin again. I noticed recently that Olo must have got tired of digging out a pit. Instead he stored the potatoes in a shed.

OTHER VEGETABLES

Apart from the cabbage, all the other vegetables were produced from seeds. They would be sown on top of readymade drills with a special mechanical sower. This would be pulled by a horse and, ingeniously, it opened a little furrow into which an attachment fed the seeds. The furrow would then be closed by a little roller which fitted snugly over the drill, pressing down lightly and closing the soil over the seeds. There were

Sower in Foleys Forge

different designs of this equipment: An old one that I have has the convex roller, which fitted down snugly over the drill, at the back. The one in the illustration has it on the front. When the plants emerged and were fit for handling we thinned them out so that there would be the required spacing between each one. We also removed weeds as we moved along the drills. This was a hands and knees job. Weed control during the growing was by scuffling and sometimes by doing a bit of hand weeding.

As for the cabbage, young plants were dug into the drills and left to their own devices except for the scuffling, although we sometimes sowed seed and thinned the plants out when they were well established. Very frequently the scuffling did not work fully, and that was when Pat and I had to travel miles on our knees removing the weeds by hand. It was depressing to be looking down a long drill, thinking you would never get to the end of it. This was a job we found difficult to extract any fun from. Fortunately Dad was not unduly particular about the quality of the work and sometimes weeds escaped with a trampling. At harvest time turnips, mangolds and the sugar beet were snagged before storage. 'Snagging' was the removal of soil around the roots with a big knife. You also cut off the leafy upper growth. Carrots and parsnips were simply pulled when mature.

The mangolds, turnips, sugar beet (we didn't process this for sugar production) and sometimes the potatoes, were mangled in a Mangler before feeding to the livestock. The mangler was basically a giant chipper. The vegetables were thrown in, the handle got a few vigorous turns and the chips dropped into a bucket underneath.

Mangler in Foleys Forge

FLAX

I have no recollection of the sowing of flax but I imagine it did not differ from the method of sowing grain. I do remember that we did not grow it on our own land. We rented a big field from the Drumlerry Sheridans. I understood that it was a very demanding crop which could leave the land somewhat impoverished. The poisoning of eels in the bog drain in which the flax was soaked was a memorable aspect of this crop.

Soaking was part of the harvesting of this cash crop during the war. A few of the farmers around grew the flax for two or three years, including Dad. The raw flax would be sold to linen weavers in Northern Ireland. We took our flax over to Munterconnaught to soak it in bog drains. I think that there was some suggestion that the flax cured better in acidic water. Interestingly, when we went to recover the flax we found many eels, large and small, dead or dying, on or about the flax. We did not know what toxicity the eels had absorbed from the flax and we regretfully left them to rot when we removed it from the bog for drying on the farm.

Flax was a labour-intensive crop, requiring cutting by scythe. After removal from the soaking process, it was spread on the field until it was again dry. We then collected it, loaded it and shipped it off. All of the process was done by hand because there was no machinery at that time, not even a horse-drawn mower. Even though we were small, we children made a useful contribution to this activity.

GRASS

Sowing grass seed was a relatively rare event, but sometimes it had to be done for crop rotation reasons. If barley, for instance, had been planted in the same field for several successive years, then a new crop had to be planted and sometimes it was grass. This new grass was always of a higher quality and yield than old meadow. The sowing was done in a similar manner to grain sowing. This field would then be reserved for hay, for a number of years at least. First crop hay would be reserved for the horses because of its superior quality.

HAYMAKING

Haymaking could be a pressurised job because of weather uncertainties. If the weather was good and the outlook settled it could be an enjoyable activity. It was not heavy work, except for the scythesman Bosheen, but the day or days would be passed in constant activity. The Bosheen would scythe away all day, leaving rows of grass behind him. The next or the

Horse-drawn Rake courtesy of Joan Mullen

following morning we would all get our forks out and walk alongside the rows turning them over so that the sun and wind could cure and dry them. When the hay was ready Dad would rake these single rows into bigger rows with the horse drawn rake. We, his sweating children, used make jokes about Dad always having the easy and interesting jobs!

Olo would then yoke up the horse to the hay gatherer or sweeper, and collect the hay in the rows to deposit it at convenient points for cock building. The hay gatherer (we called it 'the tumbler') was a wooden implement about two metres wide with flat teeth about one and a half metres long running from a beam flat along the ground. From the beam there rose uprights and two handles. It was a bit like the back of a cupped hand. When this contraption was pulled along the ground by the horse it collected the hay in the rows until it could not take any more, at which point Olo tumbled it over, releasing the hay in a

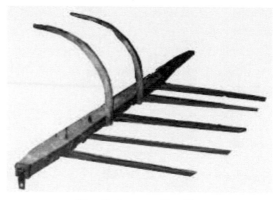

Hay Gatherer or Tumbler

heap. He would pull maybe three loads to one spot, enough to make a cock. We children would then help Dad or Paddy Mack to build a cock and so on throughout the field.

The next day, when the cocks would have settled a bit overnight, we little ones got a job we disliked very much: 'gibbing' (Irish 'giobadh') the cocks. This was our word to describe pulling out the hay at the bottom of the cock so that when it rained the little gap created by so doing ensured that the water did not land on the hay on the ground and by capillary action wet much of the lower part of the cock. The pulled out hay was placed on top of the cock as a kind of capping, and two ropes, connected to twisted hay at the bottom of the cock, tied the hay firmly together.

The ropes were wound from the base of the cock – one child would pull out, and continue pulling out with a twisting motion, a short handful of hay at the bottom without separating it from the cock. This would then be connected to a hook at the end of a short piece of bull wire shaped like an old fashioned brace. The second child would wind and wind the hay into a rope ('súgán') long enough to go over the complete cock. The problem our little hands had with this job was that there were always thistles in the hay and we never wore gloves. You could imagine what our hands would be like after a day doing that.

The hay would be saved at the end of June or in early July depending on weather and growth rates. Towards the end of August the hay would be taken from the fields and carted or pulled to the barn for winter storage. Methods of transport were basically two: by shifter or by pulling the cock along the ground with a chain.

Hay Shifter from the Ulster American Folk Park
http://www.nmni.com/uafp/Collections/Transport/Irish-Transport/Hay-Cart

The shifter, or bogey as it is called elsewhere, is a long flat cart, five or six feet wide by about ten long with a winch at the front. A chain, with a flat piece about a foot long inserted in it, would encircle the cock at ground level, the flat piece at the furthest point, and the cock would be winched on to the pre-tipped cart. If the cocks were small, two could be taken on board, and probably a half dozen children. This was the part of farming that the children loved: we clambered on to the shifter, we climbed up to the top of the cock(s) and cheered and sang and waved at passersby. We enjoyed the return journey to the field nearly as much.

Pulling the cock all the way from the field to the barnyard was an option that was taken occasionally when there was a threat of rain and it became urgent to get all the hay in and secure. The chain was placed around the cock as for the shifter and, amazingly, it could be dragged without loss all the way out of the field and up the road to the barnyard. Throwing the hay up, forkful by forkful, was hard, dusty work which was generally left to adults or bigger boys. Only an experienced hand was allowed to build the hay in the barn, but if this person was working at the far side then the younger ones would form a relay to get the hay to him.

When I hear my children reminiscing about farm holidays, bringing in the hay is always at the top of the popularity stakes. Even as recently as the sixties, our shifter was in use. All that is left of it now is the axle and wheels.

Olo entertaining visiting family, Ballinvalley 1968

FARMING WITH ANIMALS

Peter Oliver Tuite 1968

This is the livestock we had on the farm: an ass; two horses – we always bought foals and broke them in ourselves; several cows and calves and bullocks (steers); many sheep; pigs, including at least two farrowing sows; a few goats, which devoured the few flowers and other garden shrubbery we had about the place; geese, turkeys, ducks and guinea fowl – this last more for decoration than utility. There were also, of course, cats and dogs, including greyhounds. The gander that I remember was a contrary fellow who ran at us hissing if we went near him. Maybe all ganders were contrary, but in any event we little ones gave him a very wide berth. Mrs Willis from Knockbrack, where Pat was farmed out during the time I was in the Tanyard, had frightened us once by saying that the gander, if we didn't keep away from him, would bite our willies off!

Jottings of a Country Boy

A livestock farmer is primarily a facilitator of breeding activity which expands the herd or flock. The cow is taken to the bull, has a calf or calves, and produces milk for the calves and the household. The sow is taken to the boar, the she-goat to the buck, the mare to the stallion. The ram shares the field with the ewes, the cocks with the turkeys and hens, the gander with the geese and the drake with the ducks. All this interaction results in piglets, kids, foals, lambs, hen and turkey chicks, goslings, and ducklings and eventually cash flow! Birthings have to be monitored and the young protected. Lambing time was particularly demanding, especially if there was snow about. As with calving, full time attendance was required. The girls made up bottles for ailing or orphaned lambs and delighted in feeding them. Sometimes an orphaned lamb became a pet, but beware pet rams!

The geese and the turkeys, a one-off crop for the Christmas market were lavished with care because of the importance of getting some money in for that occasion. The turkeys especially got little delicacies, such as tender nettle shoots, picked by hand and cooked. The geese ate mostly grass with a little supplement added coming up to Christmas. Mangled turnips, mangolds and sugar beet would be mixed, in the winter, with a bit of meal and fed to the cows, sheep and pigs.

The sheep had to be dagged at least once a year. Dagging, kind of like snagging the turnips, was the removal of dung which, over a period of time, builds up around the sheep's tail. The sheep were susceptible to foot rot and this also needed treatment annually. Then we had the backbreaking sheep shearing which we were glad to leave to Olo once we had caught the sheep for him. Before shearing we would have dipped the sheep well, as washed wool fetched a slightly better price. For this job we borrowed the Kavanaghs' sheep dip. They had a rectangular underground tank located close to The Inny. (The river went under the road and into Kavanaghs' field from ours.) A small trench was dug from The Inny to feed the tank and the sheep were walked the length of the tank and out the opposite end. Wool would be loaded up and carted in to Charlie Gibney without delay and he would have lorry loads going off to the wholesalers.

These ministrations involved a lot of chasing and handling of sheep, mostly by us, the young and fleet footed. Dad loved having us around when those jobs came up.

Sheep and pigs would be taken to the monthly market held in The Square. The market was always interesting because there were travelling vendors enlivening the scene. It was always on a Friday and the fishmonger with the herrings, McGovern from Kells, never missed attending. It was a very social gathering as well as a serious business, was the market.

The fair, which was held mostly in the Fair Green, with some cattle also shown on the streets, was entirely different, at least for me on the occasions that we had cattle to sell, because Pat and I would be left standing in the muck, minding the cattle while Dad would be off doing deals. He would return occasionally with a potential purchaser and after many false dawns a deal would be struck. This dealing was not a straightforward affair with a 'take it or leave it' mentality. Oh no! There would be the shaking of heads, the slapping of hands, the walking away and return with a final offer, and then another 'final' offer, the rejections and finally the acceptances, sometimes with the aid of a third party who ostensibly had no axe to grind, confirmed by dipping a stick in the mud and touching a bullock's rump with it.

Meantime, I would be standing there all morning, learning a little, I suppose, but very impatient to see an end to all the posturing which the participants seemed to enjoy. Many of Dad's cattle-dealing friends would be making detours now and again to the pub for their socialising, but Dad stayed on the street to talk to people. I would be glad, in the end, to walk back home (the cattle were walked into the fair), to sit down with a nice book if I was lucky. If I had the energy later on in the day I would go out and sit on the wall where I had a grandstand view of the horses taking their merry owners home! The turkeys, geese and ducks were killed, plucked and taken to the Dublin Market after the war, but during the war, since we had no truck, we must have disposed of them locally.

OTHER JOBS

WATER FROM THE WELL

One of my regular tasks was to fetch water from the well. The well was at the far end of the home field, something under half a mile away. This day I was carrying two big buckets. (At the age of eight or nine that was hard, but I think I was just showing off). I was within one hundred yards of the house when *thump* I got this shocking blow on my behind from behind! My two precious buckets of water splashed all over me and around me. I looked around to find the cause. There it was, a playful young ram, a previous pet, getting ready to thump me again. He did get me – it's like being hit with a log. Then I managed to punch him on the nose and he backed off. I'm afraid the first thump drew a surprised swear out

Water from the Well by Rory Bjornegard Tuite (11)

of me, a swearword not appropriate for an eight- or nine-year-old, nor indeed for a seventy-nine year old. One of my sisters heard it and ran to tell my mother – not about the thumping, but about the swearing. Mam was on my case when I went in, and my misery was compounded. Off I had to go again, but this time deflated down to one bucket and a stout stick.

To the Buck by Ailbhe Reilly-Tuite (14)

A VISIT TO THE BUCK

Another recurring job I had was more interesting and required more energy. Every year, from about the age of seven or eight, I got a message from Mrs Blaney up the road to take her she-goat to the he-goat, as it was 'the time'. Now, from a young age, taking the cow to the bull, the sow to the boar was a normal activity. We didn't breed our horses, so thankfully I never had to get involved in that. But an in-heat she-goat is a mighty eager creature, and my job was to put a lead on her and take her over a few fields for about a mile to the upper end of the Summerbank Road where we visited the buck belonging to the Tobins.

While the goat and the buck were getting acquainted I would visit my namesakes, the two Miss Tuites who lived close by. They were a gentle pair, one of them being a 'spoilt' nun.   I think we and they may have been distantly related. Anyway, I got coddled up physically and mentally with delicacies and chat.

But we haven't got there yet, the goat and I – and it was the goat that was in charge! That goat pulled and dragged me at a gallop over the fields, tail wagging, tongue out maybe, (mine would certainly be out by the time we arrived). She jumped up on the walls and down the other side before I had a chance to climb up, and if the lead was not long enough I got banged against the wall. I knew it was a situation full of humour because I could see poor Mrs Blaney almost bursting with the need to laugh as I headed off. The return journey was much more sedate, except that now I had to do the pulling and dragging.

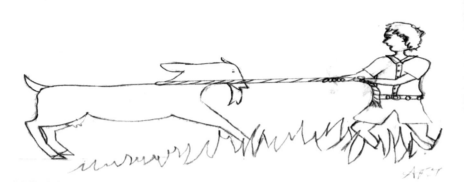

Homeward Bound by Ailbhe Reilly-Tuite (14)

A KID BY BICYCLE

An indication of how difficult things were during the 1939-45 war was that as little as five shillings (euro twenty five cents) could represent the difference between feeding well or poorly. I remember in the early 40s getting the task of taking a kid goat into town by bicycle, one hand holding the handlebar and the other clutching the kid under my oxter. The buyer, Sean McGinn's father, a keen appreciator of the culinary merits of kid, gave me five shillings for it (not for me of course). The 'poor man's cow' was plentiful in Ireland among cottagers and other rural dwellers who had no cow or only one cow. (A cow does not produce milk all year round so sometimes the period between going dry and calving would be goat's milk time).

Selling the Kid by Rebecca Bjornegard Tuite (13)

A Greyhound by Horseback

My Uncle Johnny, the second oldest of my father's siblings, made his living buying and selling greyhounds, and betting on them and on horses. He seemed to get by quite well. I suppose because of his influence my father became an owner in a major way. At one time he had up to 60 greyhounds in outhouses. They barked, seemingly all night, causing many sleepless hours. They were not loveable creatures, and everyone but my Dad would have been happy to have seen the end of them long before that actually happened. As far as I can recollect, the only profitable one was a dead one, accidentally killed on the road, for which he got £60 compensation.

At my father's request, I set out one day on horseback – I think I may have been in my twelfth year – with a greyhound on a lead, to deliver it to a Mr Stack, a schoolteacher in Maghera. This little hamlet is about ten kilometres away on the borders of Meath and Cavan. This ride, as were all my rides over the years, was bareback, as we never ever considered buying a saddle. On the way I passed 'The Bull' Tuite's farm in Munterconnaught, close to the place of origin of some of my nineteenth century ancestors. I also crossed the nine-eyed bridge over the river Blackwater as it emerges from Lough Ramor.

I got there eventually. Mr Stack was a Kerryman, very open and friendly. He allowed his amusement to show – he thought it an interesting (hilarious?) way to have a greyhound delivered. I was sat down at table and plied with many delicacies, and questions that indicated an interest as strong as my Aunt Rita's. I think he found me a bit unresponsive due to dad's admonitions about 'gabbing' about family business. After a decent interval, I signalled my intention to get back on Bob (the horse) and find my way home. He waved me off smilingly. There was no pay for that job.

Picking Stones

My uncle Pee used give Pat and me little jobs, mostly to do with herding sheep or cattle. He had land taken around about to supplement his meagre income from his own little farm. He was ok financially as he did a bit of cattle dealing. He always paid, but sometimes we had to chase him for it!

This time, I suppose we were about ten or eleven, we got a farming job: picking the stones off a meadow. It was a huge field in after-grass which had previously been tilled, and many stones had come to the surface, necessitating the raising of the mower blades and the reduction in the crop. Anyway, on a Monday morning we yoked up Connemara, Pee's lovely little pony, and set to. (His farm was about two kilometres from ours, so we had to walk there first). We had a pre-agreed price for the job – ten shillings each. That was a lot of money in the early 40s. We thought we were pulling a stroke by getting agreement for this price!

With the optimism of youth and the foolishness of the inexperienced, we reckoned two or three days would see the job done. Six days later we dragged ourselves home, our pockets hot with the lovely coloured ten shilling notes. In the door we went, waving our riches in the air and accepting our mother's praise. But not for long: "Boys", she said, "We haven't any money to pay Paddy, would you mind letting me have the pound". By this time I hope that Paddy was not still on a guinea a week. "Aw", we both muttered before handing over. We were a little downcast but willing enough to part with the fruits of our week's labours. We were doing our bit. Anyway, what would we do with ten shillings – didn't we have everything we wanted? We couldn't eat any more food than we were already eating, we were loved and appreciated and looked after. That sounds very philosophical: is there likelihood that time has distorted the memory, and that in fact these thoughts were our Mother's spoken words?

HELPING IN THE SLAUGHTER HOUSE.

I have no recollection of either Dad or Uncle Pee talking about their young days, apart from a reference Dad once made about running messages for the British soldiers. Apparently the soldiers were confined to barracks a lot and if they wanted a letter posted they had to engage the services of local youngsters. They would give the boys a penny – a halfpenny for the stamp and a halfpenny for the boys themselves. According to Dad, the boys used to put the letters in the post unstamped and buy sweets with the penny.

Sometime in their youth Dad and Pee must have learned how to kill a pig and to process the carcase. They had a little slaughterhouse in the old tanyard where they killed pigs for the many households in the parish that wished to have their own bacon. These people would have their own home-grown pigs but they either couldn't or wouldn't kill them themselves. A few times, a very few times, I was press-ganged into helping them during a slaughtering session when other help was unavailable. When I reflect on this activity, I have to keep reminding myself that I was only eight or nine at the time.

The procedure was that the pig was brought in, a chained hook was attached to its snout, and I took a hold of the chain at the loose end. When I pulled the chain the pig instinctively pulled against me, thus holding its head steady for the coup de grâce. This was delivered with a mallet with a hammer on one side and a hollow steel spike on the other. The aim was for the spike to enter the brain; if the blow was accurate it was instant death. The throat was then quickly cut and I had the task of holding a basin underneath the flow of blood. To prevent it congealing I then had to stir, and keep stirring, until it was cool. The blood would be used to make black puddings. The carcase was then lifted into a large vat of very hot water where it remained long enough to soften the bristles for scraping off. This done, the carcase was hung up, and cutting up and deboning followed.

The charge for the butchering varied. A lot depended on the liquidity of the customer. If money was a problem a deal was done on the basis that some money would pass and defined sections of meat would be retained by the butchers. We always had choice pork steaks in the house on butchering weeks!

Some people salted and hung their bacon for storage. We always salted all but the steaks and a little bit of ham and laid it piece by piece in a large wooden box on the floor of the scullery. Pieces of the pig in one form or another formed part of our daily diet. Very often when we returned from school there would be a pan full of potatoes and turnips or cabbage, fried in grease from the rashers that accompanied them. Not these days regarded as a healthy diet, but we thrived on it. Our breakfast would be porridge from our own oats, and bread mostly from our own wheat or oats. Our butter was mostly from our own churn.   We were an independent republic on our little farm! We children did not drink tea or coffee, just milk from our own cows. So during the war, and for a while after, when rationing restricted the supply of these items, we always had a cupboard full of tea and coffee. We distributed much of these rations to our non-farming family members.

Occasionally we got food from Uncle Packy that was unavailable south of the border during the war. He had business contacts and opportunities in the North and he went up there fairly regularly. Bread baked from our own wheat, while nourishing, was a bit unpalatable. We could recognise it by the ring of dark dough all around the loaf, just under the crust. Once, Packy gave us a loaf from the North and it was white, fluffy and tasty. He also brought us a stone bag of dessert rice towards the end of the war, something we had not seen since 1939. That was a big treat for us young ones and we had rice coming out of our ears for the next couple of weeks!

CAREFREE SCHOOLDAYS

MIDNIGHT MASS

We little children loved midnight mass in Oldcastle on Christmas Eve. It was a pageant, incorporating a torch-lit procession up the town, around the square and back down to the church again. It was led by the local brass band playing hymns, and the whole congregation, (those of them still able to walk anyway,) followed, led by the children. The oil-fired torches added a touch of the surreal to the atmosphere. Then, at the consecration, Oliver Burns blew the trumpet three times, a sound we little ones waited for expectantly.

The church would be packed and youngsters would be fainting through lack of air, including myself once. Part of the thrill afterwards was that we got to stay up after midnight in an extra-lively house because of the more relaxed holiday atmosphere and the ongoing preparations for the Christmas dinner. Dad would be pulling the tendons from the turkey's legs and mixing the brandy butter for the pudding, perhaps not in that order. Olo, or Eddie before he went working for Packy, would have plucked and cleaned out the turkey and goose beforehand. (We all participated in the plucking of the turkeys and geese for the market. It was a job we didn't enjoy). Mam would be preparing the trifle, boiling the pudding and undertaking a myriad of other tasks to ensure that Christmas Day would be an enjoyable occasion.

The following morning, regardless of what the weather would be like, all the boys would head off for the Sturracheen with the dogs, to work up an appetite for dinner. By a long-standing tradition we always had turkey, ham and goose, all reared on the farm. As far back as I can remember we had these three items for Christmas dinner, even in our poorest days. Neither my Mam nor Dad was a drinker, but on Christmas day they would have a glass of sherry, or in the unlikely event that there was some in the house, a glass of wine. None of our family frequented pubs or drank alcohol during their teenage years.

THE WAKE

Another interesting memory is of being delegated to attend the wake of a neighbour in Stonefield, as the rest of my family was committed elsewhere. I was about ten or eleven at the time. It was a fascinating experience. First of all there were lots of goodies and fizzy drinks, so I am sure I was rightly spoiled. I sat listening to the neighbours talking about cattle, pigs, sheep, hens, turkeys, geese, everything except women and death, with only an occasional reference to the man that had been in that body there. It seemed that death was very much a part of ordinary life.

WARTS, WELLS AND HOT POKERS

Warts were a bit of a problem in the 1930s and the 1940s, as genuine cures were difficult to come by. The most common and accepted cure was to dip the wart in wells recognised as having 'the cure'. Some people claimed to have got rid of warts that way, but I was sceptical. Sure, I have dipped a warty knee and a warty knuckle into Mrs Gilsenan's wart well, but I do not recall a cure from that source. (My recollection of this wart 'well' was that it was merely a rock with a hole in it, filled from a tiny spring. There was a cure that was certain and I had first-hand experience of it. One day in 1941 when I was seven I went to the forge in Knockbrack with Dad. He had asked me to accompany him. This was slightly unusual and I found out why after we had left the horse with the farrier and walked up the road a bit to a house that I knew well. I did not know it until afterwards, but the owner, I think he was Michael Grace, had a reputation as a destroyer of warts. I had two big ones on one of my knees. There was chat for a while and then my father casually mentioned the warts to this man. Just as casually, the man said "Oh! I think I can cure those". Unsuspecting, I sat there while he went off for something. When he returned he had a red hot poker in his hand. If my father had not reassured me I would have been out the door! Sure enough, he applied the poker to the warts. They sizzled as they burnt away and I managed to suppress my groans, which were more in expectation that the procedure was going to be extremely painful than because I was suffering. It was only when he got towards the end of the burning that I jumped off the chair with the pain. It really was not cruel, it only seemed that way! I don't think that I had any more warts after that.

The Knockbrack farrier, Johnny Haigh, was more than a farrier. It was certain that he assembled cart wheels pre-made by a carpenter. I watched him and a couple of helpers assemble a wheel, perhaps even on this visit. The key to successful assembly was a stone template laid on the ground composed of individual triangular shaped stones in a circle, with a space between each stone and a hollow centre. The spokes were placed between the stones and the hub went in the centre. The premade iron rim was then placed around the lot. This was subjected to heat to expand it and then to cold water to contract it when it was in place. This was not easily achieved, but I forget what caused the difficulty. I know it was always a struggle, as it is for my memory to offer a clear picture from long ago. Anyway, I enjoyed taking the horses to the forge and meeting different people there.

A CHARMED LIFE

Sometime in the mid-war years the council workers were lowering the level of Caldergate Hill, just outside our front gate. The only aid to the workers' muscle energy was a horse and cart for removals or delivery. This was a big manual job. In the process they encountered a huge rock some feet under the surface. It was in the centre of the new road. With pick and shovel the workers had managed to remove soil from around the rock to a depth of around two and a half meters. They then tackled the rock with sledgehammers. For several days they had been pounding away with only limited success. One frosty morning, as I set out on the bicycle to count the cattle on the mountain field, they were starting on it again. On my return down the hill the brakes failed. (They were operated by pushing backwards on the pedal and they sometimes malfunctioned in frost). I sped down the hill, round the bend by the skin of my teeth and plunged straight into the cavity around the rock, missing a worker on the way. The ganger, Terry the Garner, screamed "Oh my God, the child is dead!" I wasn't. I was hanging in the hole, head down, a foot caught in the bike frame which was holding me up. I didn't have a scratch, nor did I have any bad reaction, as at that age I thought I was immortal!

NEDDY THE DONKEY GOES ON STRIKE

Neddy was a little black nosed donkey that seemed to be around during all our young days. We all had so much fun catching him first of all and then, in turn, hopping on his back for a gallop. He would behave impeccably for the first two or three riders, going at a steady gallop. With subsequent riders he would accelerate to top speed and after about twenty metres he would lower his head and come to a sudden stop. This always had the effect of dumping his rider, sometimes painfully, on to the turf. He would then trot off kicking his heels and braying as if to say, 'Who's the ass now"?

Once there was a group of smaller children in the yard and they persuaded me that I should take them for a ride in Neddy's cart. The old cart had had inflated wheels but now the tyres were missing and the cart's wheels were on the rim. This made it difficult to pull. Off up the mountain lane we went with Neddy going from side to side to reduce the slope and showing little enthusiasm for the task. He continued on for a couple of hundred yards, stopping now and again, presumably in protest. Suddenly, he collapsed and lay deathly still on the road. I rushed to release the pulling chains and to remove the shafts of the cart from him. As soon as he felt released from the shafts he scrambled to his feet and took off braying and giving an occasional flick of his heels. I swear, if a donkey can laugh, he was doing it merrily. I had no option but to pull the cart full of children home, much to their amusement. Fortunately it was mostly downhill.

On another occasion, our neighbour Pee Farrelly asked me to yoke up Neddy and go with him to Fennor to collect something. Fennor is on the Ballyjamesduff side of Oldcastle, about three miles from Ballinvalley. It must have been after the event with the rimless cart because the one that I yoked Neddy up to this time had the traditional wooden wheels with iron rims, and a two-foot-high crib. Pee set off ahead of me on his bicycle going at a pace which maintained a distance of about fifty metres between us.

Neddy was doing well, trotting briskly, without tantrum. When we got to the other side of town, Pee sped up a bit, so I urged Neddy into a gallop. In my imagination I was a heroic charioteer charging the enemy (I had been reading again). We had got quite close to Pee when he suddenly took a sharp turn left on to a minor road. We tried to follow.

Neddy managed to get around the turn, but the cart and I didn't make it. The left wheel hit the banked corner edge and the cart began to accelerate into a roll. I leaped away from it and, propelled by the overturning cart, landed in a drain in the field on the opposite side of the narrow road. The cart landed with a clatter, top end down. When I managed to extricate myself from the drain, scrambling to view the disaster, there was Neddy on his back, legs waving in agitation, still between the shafts which were now almost flat on the road. Pee was coming into view, fear that I might be under the cart etched on his face. He was shouting "Peter, Peter, are you all right"? When he saw me emerging from the drain his first reaction was huge relief; his second was to make the air around us blue with his choicest expressions. These left me in no doubt about my origins and other things that I need not mention! We managed to right the cart and Neddy, and we proceeded on our way rather more sedately, luckily without injury or damage to man or beast.

A DARING ROBBERY AT KATIE GROWNEYS

Katie Growney, a fairly elderly lady, lived at the other side of the 'Bottoms' in a little cottage which was in reality a bit of a hovel. Despite her obvious poverty and possibly a slight eccentricity, she was generous with her time and her little bits of food when we visited, so we never skipped her if we were passing that way. Katie churned her own butter. She didn't churn too often and the butter from the previous churning often went off. We must have been unlucky that the fresh butter was never available. Her standard fare was a slice of soda bread *plastered* with butter. We, of course, accepted the gift with good grace, but we became adept at pretending to eat it and managing to dispose of it out the door or window when she was not watching.

One day she was rushed off to hospital, leaving requests to some man known to her to look after the place in her absence. On a Monday morning shortly thereafter, two policemen darkened our door looking for Peter Tuite. Sergeant Reynolds was one and the other was, I think, Guard Aherne. They asked me where I was 'last Sunday'. Now, this was just Monday and yesterday was yesterday, so last Sunday to my little mind was the previous Sunday. Could I account for my movements last Sunday? Of course not, I couldn't remember anything I had done on that day! "Well", said Sergeant Reynolds, "were you in Katie Growney's last Sunday"? As it happened, I had been there during the previous fortnight, before she went to hospital, but I was a bit frightened and confused and I said I could not remember. They measured my feet and went away without explanation, saying they would be back. I was scared, having visions of 'the Black Hole' which they had mentioned casually during the interview. At my age, I and all my age group, believed that there was such a thing in every police station and that once in there, you never got out.

Several hours later they returned with the news that Paddy McCann had said that I had been in Katie Growney's last Sunday and that I had stolen a turkey egg and a pound of butter from her house; that they would be back for me and I had better be ready to confess all. That really put me into a frenzy of fear and my poor mother began to clean me up and put slightly better clothes on me for my visit to the barracks. It appeared that they had, in true Sherlock Holmes fashion, found a barefoot print in the vicinity of Katie's home which indicated someone of my age. I was frozen with fright for the remainder of that day, the image of the 'Black Hole' becoming more and more terrifying. The following morning, after a sleepless night, I was prepared for the worst. The fear was numbing. Then around noon a neighbour came in saying "Have you heard about ___ He's been arrested for a robbery at Katie Growney's. Apparently he has confessed".

We learned later that the Guards had called on a number of boys, telling each one that another had accused him of the crime until the unfortunate guilty one confessed. The Guards did not return to ease our fears. The poor boy was prosecuted and found guilty of the crime. When Katie returned home and discovered what had happened she was enraged that her man had brought the guards in and that they had pursued the matter to the conclusion that they did.

The only positive to be gleaned from this ugly little story is that it was obvious that rural Ireland was a haven of tranquillity and peace as evidenced by the fact that the Garda had no greater crime to solve. Two policemen spent two days getting their 'man', and probably another day on paperwork plus time in court, all for a rotten turkey egg and a pound of rancid butter! For the same reason, two guards would spend a half a day measuring, chain by chain, the distance from the Pub to Neddy Boylan's house even though they already had it on file. As for me, I had a couple of subdued days recovering from the trauma, but then my natural optimism resurfaced and I got over it. I was wary of Gardaí and their methods from then. I wonder how many young lads of eight or nine have confessed to crimes they did not commit?

DILLY GOES SHOPPING WITH A BASKET ON HER HEAD

In the 1940s, when Dilly was fifteen, she was given a five pound note to go into town for some shopping. She placed the note in a basket and set out on the two mile journey. When she was a few hundred metres from Soden's, it started to rain and, forgetting the five pound note, she put the basket on her head as protection. When the shower had passed Dilly removed the basket from her head, and to her horror the fiver was no longer there. The note had fallen out and a man cycling close behind her had picked it up and cycled off with it. He may have thought 'finders keepers' but in any event he paid for his sins, as he had been seen doing the grubby deed by some passerby. A five pound note may seem a trifling matter today, but Paddy Mack, our farm worker, would need to work for over a week for that amount. (The minimum wage by the mid-forties was just under five pounds a week). The thief was successfully prosecuted (what great Gardaí we had!). The item must have appeared in some Irish paper because some time later Uncle Mickey sent a cutting from one of the New York papers with the heading as above, "Dilly Goes Shopping with a Basket on Her Head".

A memorable moment in Dilly's life occurred when she was younger. She was walking along the top of a boundary bank which had a strand of barbed wire on top at a height of about four feet. Much of the new boundary fencing which was put in place when the land was divided was hand made by digging a ditch and piling the soil into a bank. The inner fence would then be about six feet high and the outer three feet. In effect it was almost a Ha-Ha. We always called those fencings 'the ditches'. A stranger would wonder what we were talking about when we spoke of being *on* the ditch. Dilly was holding on to the wire as she made her way forward. She slipped, a barb caught on her underarm, ripping it almost from elbow to armpit, and a gaping wound appeared. "Me guts are hanging out, me guts are hanging out!" she screamed, dashing panic-stricken into Mam. I was beside her when it happened and the wound was impressive!

ADVENTURES IN THE ORCHARD

I was for Hell for sure! I had just robbed apples from the Parish Priest's orchard. This was during the war so I must have been nine or ten. Although I had robbed many orchards I would not normally consider stealing from God's own priest Father O'Farrell. I wonder if I avoided his confessional when I confessed to stealing the apples, and if, like the sinner who confessed to stealing a rope and 'forgot' to mention the pig tied to the end of it, I also forgot to mention that it was his apples I had stolen!

However, there was a great need to be met, requiring immediate action. There was a matinee in the cinema after school and I did not have the three pence entry fee, nor did I have time to run two miles home and two miles back to get it. 'Johnny Mack Brown', our favourite cowboy at the time, was not going to be missed! There was a ready market among my classmates for the apples and I sold them in two lots at two pence each. That left me with a penny for sweets. I really enjoyed screaming with the other two hundred children "Come on, Johnny Mack Brown!" or "Watch out behind you!" when the hero was chasing the villain or being chased.

Our favourite orchards were Red Paddy's and Mrs Soden's. Red Paddy Sheridan lived with his brother down through 'the Bottoms' and onwards across the fields to the far end of Boolies. In his orchard were the most gorgeous large red streaked apples, but there was a problem: Red Paddy had a shotgun and we were scared little boys every time we sneaked into his orchard. Sometimes, when there was the slightest sound from the house, we scattered like startled pigeons in Trafalgar Square, to reassemble again when we were reassured that he was not at a window with the gun. This man was a bit eccentric. He was a beef farmer but an unusual one in that he would never sell his bullocks until they were three years old. At that age on the plentiful grass of his fertile fields and with access to the pure water of An Eithne, they were like elephants. He was proud of them and we frequently saw him marching up and down the fields with the gun on his shoulder, saluting each bullock as he passed it by.

Mattie and Mrs Soden had an extensive orchard just a mile down the road from us, in Boolies. (Our brother Eddie in later years bought the property. It had a large house and close to two hundred acres of first class grazing land). The Sodens' apples could not compare with Red Paddy's, but they were still worth going after. Our sense of adventure when we entered the orchard was heightened by the fact that Mrs Soden was an ex-teacher and temperamental to boot. She was also reputed to have a gun but we never saw evidence of its existence. I remember sometime after the event described below doing a day's work for her and I was pleasantly surprised at how nice she was.

Anyway, this moonlit night a group of us, perhaps five in all, were up in the apple trees filling our bags when the gate to the orchard crashed open and Mrs Soden ran at us screaming. Four of us scattered, legging it as quickly out of her reach as our little legs would carry us.

The fifth one? Well, Patsy Bardon's tree overhung a chicken coop and in his terrorised haste he lost his grip and crashed on to its roof. That would have been fine had the roof not been rotten. In among the chickens he crashed with an almighty din and deafening squawks from the hens. The door was bolted from the outside, and as Patsy was quite small, his frantic attempts to climb out were in vain. He was trapped and he had to face his nemesis all on his own since there was little chance that the rest of us were going to return in support. As we waited for him chortling with nervous laughter we knew that all he would most likely get would be a prolonged telling off and vehement threats as to his fate were he to do it again. He re-joined us with a sheepish grin and we shared our booty with him. Robbing orchards in the country was tolerated and laughed about, unlike the situation around Dublin where one could very well end up in court.

Slogging Apples by Tiarnan Tuite Gilligan (11)

CHARLIE AND BENNY

Charlie Smith cycled daily into the secondary school from Rehard and as he passed us on the way home he was constantly being taunted by the smaller children with an old rhyme current at the time: "Charlie, Charlie, quack, quack, quack, went to the river with three young ducks...!

This day he was having a bad day and when Benny Monaghan shouted out the ill-advised chant without first checking what kind of humour he might be in, Charlie jumped off the bike while it was still going, leapt across the dry stone wall like Arkle, and chased Benny across Sheridan's field. Charlie was very athletic. Poor Benny didn't have a chance as he had failed to clear the wall in one go. Charlie caught him, terrified him with threats, and we heard Benny wailing "I'll never do it again, I'll never do it again". Charlie returned to his bicycle in better humour than when he left it!

But Charlie, despite his tendency to overreact to the teasing of youngsters, could just as quickly rediscover his sense of humour. Since I knew him better than some of the other Ballinvalley boys, due to the visits I had made to Rehard in my wanderings, I was pretty sure that as soon as he mounted his bicycle he had a grin on his face. In later life I played a bit of golf with him and he was always good company. He won an All-Ireland medal playing centre field for Meath in the early 1950s and by the 1970s he had built up a very successful business in textiles. His brother Mannix was working in Packy's garage when I was with Granny. I was glad to meet him a few years ago on a holiday in the Canaries, where he has a home. His funeral was today, January 18th, 2014. Benny, who made his living cattle-dealing, never left Oldcastle.

I'LL NEVER DO IT AGAIN

I imagine that this declaration of intent was heard many times in our household and elsewhere. The other of only two occasions that I remember involved my eldest brother, Eddie. He, Olo and Michael were up the field one summer day smoking Woodbine cigarettes behind a rock when Dad came on them by surprise. He had caught Eddie at it previously and he had issued dire warnings about the practice, and the punishment it would earn if he ever smoked again. Eddie was seven years older than me and he left home at fourteen, so I imagine that he must have been twelve or thirteen then. Dad was angry at Eddie, not only because he was smoking again, but also because he was leading young Olo and Michael into forbidden territory. He grabbed him, shook him and started to slap him around the legs and the bum, saying, like the comedian Bill Cosby, "Didn't I tell you not to do it again". Eddie promised in the time worn phrase: "I'll never do it again; I'll never do it again". The three of them went on to smoke for many years, Eddie fairly lightly, the other two heavily. Dad smoked on and off over the years.

This reminds me of the first time I smoked. Olo and I were snagging turnips on a cold November day. I was probably about ten and my hands were numb with the cold. Olo was still smoking the vile Woodbines and he offered me a 'pull', saying it would warm me up. I accepted the offer, inhaled sharply and spent the next few minutes coughing and spluttering and finding it hard to get breath. I did not touch a cigarette again for six years. Having a cigarette was how we celebrated a win for the college football team in Finian's! Way to go, as the Americans say! I subsequently smoked on and off until I was thirty-one.

THE HUGE TROUT

I mentioned the turf bank which we had in Roebuck during the war. One day I was returning from there by bicycle. The Inny at Castlecor was a sizeable river at this point, crossed by two bridges less than a half a mile apart. Shoals of trout were visible in this section and I could not resist the temptation to have a go at catching one. However, the water was knee-deep and there seemed to be few or no crevices or stones where the trout hid. My efforts seemed as futile as the chasing of rabbits on Sliabh na Callaigh. Being the optimist that I was and stubborn with it, I walked up and down the river for two hours, ending up soaked to the waist. I had to squat to get my hand under rocks or into crevices so that I was actually sitting in the water.

Do you make your own luck or do you just get lucky? Possibly a bit of both – because I got my fish in the end! I was just about to give up when I stood on a clump of weeds, and there, trapped under my foot, was a *monster* trout. In my excitement and my fear of losing it, I sat down in the water, carefully caught it by the gills with both hands, and stepped out on dry land as quickly as I could.

But my excitement soon abated when the size of the trout gave me a problem. How could I get through Oldcastle without someone seeing it sticking out and reporting me to the guards? My pocket was not big enough to hold it; carrying by hand was not an option, nor was sticking it down my trousers, thankfully, as I might lose it down the leg of my short schoolboy pants. In the end I wrapped it in weeds and pulled out my shirt from my waistband until I had a sizeable pouch. I popped the lot in there and cycled wetly and nervously through the town. I kind of looked the other way while I was passing the church! None of my many fishing days after that could match that day, that excitement. I hesitate to say how many meals my monster trout provided. Suffice to say that it was most enjoyable, as it was on the pan as soon as I got in the door. Mam was delighted (for me).

THE HERCULEAN TASK

I had been reading Greek mythology. The latest chapter dealt with the Twelve Tasks of Hercules, the god hero. One of these tasks impressed me more strongly than the others – although his task to go to the Western Isles to steal a herd of cattle was a close second: he clobbered many other gods on his way there and back, and in between impregnated a Celtic maiden. She had his son who was Celtis, the god of the Celts. I liked to think that he had the good sense to steal his cattle in Ireland and not enough character to resist the allure of an Irish maiden. (There are other versions of this story).

The winner, the fifth task, was to clean out the stables of some other god, a really lazy one, as the stables had not been cleaned for thirty years, and a thousand cattle were housed in them. Hercules used his head instead of his strength. There were two convenient rivers nearby which he diverted to the stables and washed them out in a day. I suppose he was ruthless enough to ignore the needs of the poor old fish!

We had a stable which housed young cattle in the winter which had not been cleaned out for about seven years. Each year a layer of straw would be spread on the floor and each winter the cattle added more nutrients until there was manure nearly seventy centimetres high in the shed which itself was about ten metres square. So, inspired by Hercules, I took on the task of removing this accumulation, but without the benefit of diverted rivers or the strength of Hercules.

The layers of manure were so matted and compacted that it was not possible to pull them apart so I used a hay knife as a cutting tool. This tool measured about five inches at the top, tapering to a point at the bottom about eighteen inches down. The cutting technique was to exert pressure on its 'T' handle from above, with a slight sideways movement. The result was a slice or a log of manure which could be gathered by fork and carted away. The fork which I used was a four pronged one. Around my part of Meath, Westmeath and Cavan, we called them 'grapes' or 'graips'. Only the two-pronged ones were called 'forks'. The word 'graip' is unknown in Dunshaughlin, as is the Oldcastle word 'shifter' for a flat-bottomed cart with a winch on it for pulling cocks of hay up on it. They call it a 'bogey' in the eastern part of Meath according to Christy Foley. In other parts of the country it is called a 'float'.

I was about nine at the time and it took me two weeks of almost daily labours to complete the task. I was delighted with myself that I had passed the self-imposed Herculean test. Even though I was strong for my age, it was tough work cutting and forking such a huge amount of manure. My Dad found me at it one day and all he said was "You'll have no grunts left for tomorrow", but I could see that he was pleased with me. He was also pleased with the fact that he would no longer be whacking his head on the roof beams. The height of the manure had brought these within head banging range! I now take great delight in hearing some of my grandchildren embellishing their physical efforts with hearty superfluous grunts!

THE 1947 BLIZZARD

When I think about this event which occurred when I was twelve, there immediately springs to mind a vision of vanished walls and roadway, and makeshift toboggans skimming down Alwell's hill field, crossing over the same invisible walls and roadway and ending up in the 'bottoms' field. The snow filled every ditch and crevice, every tree was coated in frozen snow and the landscape looked as if a white sheet had been spread on the whole earth. Temperatures as low as -26° froze the drifts to almost walkable hardness and caused the makeshift toboggans to reach exhilarating speeds. A bitter East wind kept the population indoors except for absolute necessities, and for tobogganing! Horses and cattle perished in snow drifts, lakes froze over to a depth of up to eighteen inches. There were stories of marathon journeys on foot from abandoned cars, trucks and buses, but fortunately no news of a human fatality in Meath and Cavan.

We, the Ballinvalley youngsters and teenagers were, of course, aware of hardships, and animal losses after the event. We would have seen Olo and Dad head out into the arctic conditions to attend to lambing sheep, cows and horses but we would not have thought much of it. We were carefree and all our attention was directed towards enjoying the conditions. To this end I produced my own toboggan out of a castoff petrol tank from an obsolete truck. The tank was about a metre long with a rounded bottom. We had no hacksaw so I set about cutting it in half horizontally with a hammer and chisel. The task took hours. On completion what I had was a dangerous looking, almost boat shaped, container with wickedly jagged edges. With the insouciance of youth I set off up Alwell's hill, sat into the contraption and let it take me where it willed.

The first problem arose immediately – no matter which end of it I sat in, it refused to go face forward, so there I was hanging on grimly and fearfully as I accelerated backwards down the hill at frightening speed. The fear turned to exhilaration as I skimmed over the buried walls and roadway into Phil Lynches 'bottoms' field. As I went I had a flashing view of other children on the hill until I disappeared from view in the 'bottoms'. There was not one normal toboggan in sight – everyone had used their own imagination to provide the means: planks, trays, coal bags, basins and anything else that would move on the snow. It was a long haul back up the hill, (I had never dreamed that I would one day walk over the roadway and wall without touching them) but we all had inexhaustible energy and again and again we trudged up and sped down. Of course schools were closed so we were free to spend several days at this activity in festive mood. The thaw did not happen until early April, but long before that our enthusiasm abated and only a few of us took to the 'toboggans' occasionally. My sister Maeve reminds me that our parents invited all the participants, about twenty towards the end, to a gathering in the house for hot drinks and snacks, and the house was full of cheerful chatter.

SKINNY DIPPING IN THE INNY

Occasionally, if there were enough children around and it was a hot day we would decide to go for a swim in the Inny down by the 'Bottoms', where the stream was wider than in Mack's and the bank was higher. The dam to create the swimming pool was going to be a major project requiring many helpers, especially as there was no bridge to support the structure. This dam would be about eight feet wide by four high and it required a double row of scraws to give a thickness of about two feet. Any rocks we could find would then be pressed against the back of it to give added support. We would do this several times during a good summer.

 The procedure was that a couple of the bigger boys would dig the scraws; another would stand by the dam and await the arrival of his building materials in the hands and arms of the little ones, boys and girls. He would lay the scraws, trample them down and have the 'drones' trample on them before they returned to fetch more. It was hard work because the completed dam would not last more than a half-hour after filling up and we had to keep ahead of the rising water. The flow at this point in the river was quite strong.

Jottings of a Country Boy

Finally, with much laughter and a few wetting accidents the now mud-splattered children could think of cooling off in the pool. The oldest of us would be about ten, so there was no consciousness of nakedness as we shed all our clothes and dived in. We would disport ourselves in the water and on the banks with great merriment, accompanied by much splashing and chasing.

While the dam was being built and the water supply was being cut off, the trout would start splashing, and with great discipline we would refrain from chasing them until the dam was secure. Once we had had our bit of fun and there were signs of strain on the dam, some of the boys would go after the fish, some of which were quite sizeable. It was tremendous fun. The trout, even though they were now in shallow water, were still quite elusive and difficult to hold on to, so everybody, boys and girls, joined in. There was more fun when the dam burst and you would be almost on the point of catching a big one. You would be there, hand in a crevice or under a rock, just touching the trout but not quite able to get a grip of it and there was no way you were going to let it get away, no matter what wave of water was coming at you.

We did not always succeed with our dams. Once or twice the dam breached before completion or just as the water reached its maximum height, but we always rebuilt to the point of weariness. The participants would be some or all of the Tuites, the McCanns - Paddy, Johnny, Mary, Dotie, Marcella and possibly Willie; some of the Blaneys, and the Monaghans. The Boolies Tuites were too young or not yet born to be involved in this sport in my time. The dam was normally built at the bottom of Phil Lynch's field, but I don't think Eithne and Monica ever participated.

This brings to mind another skinny-dipping event many years later when I was about twenty. We had played a game of football in the park and a few of us were loitering up town in the square. It was a pleasant balmy night. Denis McAdams joined us and suggested that we should go out to Lough Lene for a midnight swim. Five of us headed off in Denis's car (he could afford one as he was a bank clerk). We left behind in the square a small group of lads including the manager of a rival bank.

Since we had no swimwear and it was dark we were comfortable skinny dipping. We had a refreshing swim, larked about for a while, and returned to the shore for our clothes. They were gone. Denis, spotting a solitary trousers (mine) exclaimed "Bastards! They've followed us out and swiped our clothes". The 'swipers' had made the mistake of leaving my trousers out of respect for 'the Cloth'. (I was a black-clad seminarian at the time).

The four naked guys and I piled into the car and we headed back the ten miles to Oldcastle, wondering as we went where we could beg, borrow, or steal some clothes. I asked, mischievously, which of them was going to knock on someone's door bollocks-naked? There were no volunteers, so I suggested that we should stop at Caffrey's of Millbrook and I would requisition at least four trousers.

I was well known in Caffrey's, and Father Tom Caffrey had told me that when he was a young fellow and I was about two, I had turned up at their house buck-naked. (This roaming about started early!) We had moved out of 'the camp' and were living in a house down the road from Caffreys at the time. At this time in the fifties, Fr Tom was the Junior Dean in St Columhan's, Dalgan Park and I was a student there. Sure enough, Mrs Caffrey scratched around and found five old shirts and four trousers of varying sizes for my naked pals.

We proceeded towards Oldcastle. On the way we had a merry discussion about how we were going to handle the entry to the square, knowing that there would be an enlarged group standing around outside Herbstreit's door. They would be showing a complete lack of interest in the prospect of four naked young men and one half naked, emerging from a car in the middle of the square. We came slowly, hesitantly, into the square, pulled up to within fifty metres of the men just standing there, looking about them aimlessly and disinterestedly. We sat in the car watching them. Finally, Denis started the car, revved it up noisily and raced up to the pavement where our watchers were congregating. We then emerged nonchalantly from the car and strolled towards them with innocent smiles. Deignan the bank manager was the first to break the silence, "Bastards", he said, and the nonchalance and disinterest broke down into raucous laughter. Explanations were sought, as were our clothes, and both were given.

We all enjoyed the experience and over the years of frenetic city life I have remembered that there is a quality of life in small communities absent from the city. We, the swimmers, thought nothing of going off on a thirty kilometre round trip at midnight for a swim; the idlers on the square did the same trip just to play a trick and have a laugh.

MITCHING AGAIN

One wet day Pat and I joined up with Tommy Blaney, I think, and Mattie Monaghan on our way to school. The rain had been heavy for a while and there were pools of water on the roads. We were then nine-or-ten-year-olds, going on three, so we could not resist dashing into the water again and again, splashing each other until we did not have a dry stitch on us.

Facing the prospect of spending a wet and shivery day in school we discussed our options and decided that we would do the sensible thing and return home. However, on the way we got diverted by a distraction – it was to try for a trout or two under Boolies' Bridge. This took an hour or two, and at that late stage arriving home would raise a lot of questions, so we decided that we would defer homecoming until an hour which would fit in with school hours. Off we went wandering then, up along the Inny, through the swampy 'Bottoms', past Katie Growney's on the left, past our own homes on the far right until we reached the 'Flax Pool'. This was a deepish pool, fed by a spring, in which flax was sometimes soaked. We used to swim in it at one time but eventually the coldness of the water drove us to choose the Inny for our swimming.

From the flax pool we wended our way leisurely towards McCormack's farm, passing through Sheridan's, where Pat and I used find the best cow patties. We bypassed McCormack's farm and moved on to Patrickstown, known to us as 'Matt Reilly's', where one of the three Loughcrew cairns is located.

This hill is now forested, but in the 1940s it was covered in heather, berry-bearing shrubs and hazelnuts on the upper reaches, much as in Jonathan Swift's day. There were lots of rabbits too. Only the lower fields were in grass. From the top we could see in the south east the Dublin mountains and in the north east the Mountains of Mourne. Slieve Bloom and the mountains up towards Enniskillen are visible from the Sturracheen but not from Matt Reilly's. We traversed the summit of the hill to the western down-slope. This led on to our mountain field and the beginning of the Ballinvalley lane. Our long walk was interspersed with sit-down chats and occasional run-arounds chasing each other. Our timing was good as we saw children coming up the lane, so we headed home. I never mitched again.

ROMANTIC BEGINNINGS IN BALLINVALLEY
Even though boys and girls after First Class were unfortunately segregated at school, we still got opportunities, mostly through contact with the opposite sex's siblings, to get to know each other. At twelve or thirteen, even in those 'old fashioned' days, we were beginning to notice each other, but I was too shy with girls to progress matters. Girls of that age, however, were more adventurous.

One day during the summer holidays I was sitting on a wall outside my house when I saw two young girls of about my age walking up the road towards me from the direction of town. As they approached I recognised them as Eithne Lynch and Margo Kearney, and to my surprise I was the motivation for their four mile round trip. Eithne was the one showing the interest. We had a conversation for a while during which I became a bit alarmed when Eithne invited me to be her boyfriend. I wasn't yet ready for this and I somehow mumbled my way out of the difficulty without offending either girl. The upshot was that they returned to town with kind words but no commitment. Eithne and I were warm friends in our teenage years but we met infrequently and then only in public. I still have warm memories of her as the first girl to take a romantic interest in me. Poor Margo died young.

Years later, in the late seventies, there was a reunion of the pupils of the national school from the years 1943 to 1948. It was a wonderful, heart-warming, occasion. I found it to be sensational that the children I had known and pretty much taken for granted thirty-odd-years before had metamorphosed into beautiful men and women. This metamorphosis was not confined to physical features, it also embraced their characters. I luxuriated in their company.

Eithne had an almost identical twin called Monica, and in the old days I was able to tell them apart. As I was sitting taking a little break and enjoying watching these lovely strangers, ghosts of the past, I saw this vision coming towards me, a lovely graceful figure which had to be one of the twins. I made my guess and greeted her warmly "Monica"! The smile on her face became a tiny grimace and she said, slightly icily and with gritted teeth, "Eithne". Efforts at recovery were only partially successful and that was the last time I spoke to her. It is unlikely that I will get another chance to make amends. Ninety per cent of the group assembled that day had emigrated and had not met since leaving school years before. (Monica had attended my sister Maeve's wedding in Long Island).

ROAMING THE COUNTRYSIDE

Once, a small group of us – Pat, Paddy Gibney, Patsy Bardon and I – set off to wander the countryside. We had no objective in mind, just enjoying the freedom to roam. Our first visit was to the farmyard of relatives of Paddy – we called them 'The Garners'. (I think their correct name was McEnroe). It was one of these Garners who witnessed my precipitous descent into the hole in the road. While we were exploring the loft of one of the sheds, Paddy discovered an old bird's nest with an egg in it, and he promptly squashed it on the top of my head. It stank! As I was the youngest and smallest in the group, it was normal for me to be the butt of 'jokes' and other mildly bullying behaviour. The stench of that rotten egg was around me all that day.

From the Garners we continued on, past 'Blue Arsed' Gillick's house, towards Rehard, the townland of Paddy Beggan and Charlie Smith, both famous Meath footballers. It was also the townland of the Caffreys of whom the most prominent was Jimmy 'The Dump'. There was a water-powered mill there and a broad area of running water. One of Jimmy's brothers told us that if we would shuffle in a line through the water towards him, he would catch us some trout in their favourite hidey hole. Sure enough we each got one, only about eight inches long, but enough to make us happy. We went on from there doing a wide circle back towards our starting point. On the way, by road now, we came upon a large three-storey deserted house with some broken windows. Needless to say we cleared the area of throwing-stones and the house of the remaining glass. That was nice because every boy would like to have that opportunity.

We were pretty hungry by now – silte ag an ocras – but it was summer and there were no turnips available in the fields so early. (In the autumn we could stay roaming all day on the energy provided by a few turnips across some hedge). We took a shortcut through the fields to reach 'The Covert', a small wood with a variety of fairly mature trees. It was probably the only decent stand of trees on the Ballinvalley side of Oldcastle, other than Sheridan's lawns. There were a few birds there, and traces of foxes, badgers and rabbits. Suddenly there was a noisy flapping of wings, and a largish odd-shaped bird flew off into the adjoining field and settled on the grass about seventy five yards away. To our surprise and delight it was an owl, a rare sight in this treeless landscape. Now, Paddy Gibney was rated in the area for his accuracy with stones. He asked us if he should hit the owl, and we voted no. He threw the stone anyway, and injured the bird to the extent that we were able to approach it and pick it up. He wanted to put it out of its misery, but I held onto it and said, "I'll take it home and nurse it back to health". However, it died on the way, and I was accused of killing it. Paddy emigrated to England. We never saw him again. Not far from home, a neighbour was standing at his gate, and he noticed us carrying the trout. His offer of a shilling each was too good to resist, and we went off home grinning.

BLEST

"I'm blest" is the answer I always get from a friend when I greet him. He has nothing but his guitar, his faith and a positive attitude. I also was blest in all aspects of my boyhood. Blest in my immediate and extended family; blest in my neighbours, especially in all those extraordinarily kind and lovable women; blest in my teachers and blest in my friends of long ago. I hope that I have managed to communicate this in the little stories as they unfold, and that some of them may touch the heart of the reader and bring back happy memories.

JOTTINGS OF A COUNTRY BOY
1948 - 2014

"I would like to hear your life as you heard it coming at you...I would like to hear it as it sounded while it was passing".   Wallace Stegner

ADOLESCENCE AND EDUCATION

In St Finian's College Mullingar in early September 1948 we, the first year students, on our first day, were shuffling around in an open area surrounded by groups of second and third years, a threatening presence to the nervous newcomers. We were being branded with nicknames. We bore a strong resemblance to calves in a Wild West corral. The branding iron was the wit and powers of observation of the older boys applied with relentless cruelty. I was called 'Chesty', Jerry Bellew was 'Jelly Belly'!

We were to learn very soon that the teachers were not immune to nickname attachment either. Jimmy Grehan, the Greek teacher, was called 'Caligula' after the diminutive and cruel Roman Emperor whose favourite pastime appeared to be kicking his pregnant wife in the belly. Dick Teahan, the Irish teacher, was very subtly called Dick. Fr Abbott was called a very unsubtle Bud. Our science teacher, Mr O'Brien, was called 'The Muss' – I don't know why. Fr Flynn, our Latin teacher, had the name 'Beano' as he was a voracious reader. (His favourite dictum was "Delenda est carelessness" – down with carelessness)! Jane Austin put her finger on it when she wrote "For what do we live but to make sport for our neighbours and laugh at them in our turn"? We discovered quickly that we were called 'Guffs'. The Urban Dictionary definition of guff is "a cloud of foul gas left hovering in the air after some bastard has farted". Fortunately we had no idea of this meaning, thinking in our innocence that it was some fancy Greek word for 'innocents abroad' or some such.

The immediate need for us young ones was to find some kindred spirits that we could associate with comfortably in this foreign and not-so-benign environment, judging by first impressions at least. Groups of two, three, four, and in my case, five, formed within a day or so in a fairly haphazard fashion. My group was composed of: Mick Lynn from Ballinacarragy, Kieran Dunican from Ardcath, Tom McDonnell from Crossakiel, Jim Ryan from Ballinlough, just over the hill from Ballinvalley and myself. For the next five years we stayed intact, walking around the walks day after day during those free periods too short to do anything else, such as football or handball. Since we were not allowed to read the newspapers or listen to the radio (if we had one), our conversation would not be grounded on a free flow of information. We became good school friends, but when we dispersed out into the great wide world in 1953, all contact ceased as we went our different routes.

So, with chest out and chin up I tackled the problems of survival in this strange community. The first thing that struck me was that nobody in this place cared a hoot for me. It was a community of largely egocentric individuals who appeared to be as cold as the metal in the bells that were to boss us about for the next five years. For some months I lay sleepless night after night listening to the haunting hoot of a foghorn out in the bog where the trains slowed down because of the mists. I had plenty of time to regret having chosen to wrench myself from the bosom of my family and the warm embrace of a caring community. At the same time I knew that I would be well served by the same pragmatism with which I and all my family had faced the more serious difficulties of the Economic War, and WW2 which came hot on its heels. I had not forgotten how to cope.

I merged into the community, paid attention in class, amazingly managed to study and produce homework off my own bat, indulged in frenzied activity on the football field as often as I could and generally got on well with pretty well everyone. I felt unhappy about the dominant role the bell played in my life, often wishing that I could be getting a cuff on the ear from my mother, rather than a ding-dong from a piece of metal. It was a funny life, a funny year. I cannot piece together any detailed good memories of 1948/49. This was unlike all the clear memories I had of my boyhood days when I was happy, free and carefree. Perhaps I can attribute this to the fact that my days and even years in Finian's could be described as remotely happy - happiness seen through a mist like the one out on the bog, but dissipating in your hands when you tried to grasp it. That did not mean that I went around with a long face. In our self-focused world we all became adept at concealing our feelings.

I do have two dark memories of incidents which occurred during my first year. One was a triviality blown up to serious proportions by Larry Fagan, our President; the other was serious.

We were absolutely forbidden to be out of our dorms once lights were out and it was a brave boy who would chance it as there was an occasional night patrol. One Sunday night I did brave the corridor to get to Coach Jim Deignan's room for the GAA results. Standing outside his door you could just about hear the radio. Everything was going fine until Larry Fagan himself appeared from nowhere, sucked in his breath in disapproval and spent a few minutes satisfying himself that I was not up to anything else. Even so, the word expulsion was mentioned a few times and I went back to my dorm in some agitation. I would not have put it past the same Larry Fagan to carry out his threat. Anyway, he adopted a softer attitude the following day and all was well.

The second incident was much more serious. In the spring of 1949 I was collared on a deserted corridor by two seniors. One of them, a fellow called Macken, grabbed me, pinioned my arms by my sides and wheeled me around to face the other, 'The Bish' Conroy. Apparently he had received some misinformation, or indeed possibly malicious information, that I had revealed in class to Dick Teahan what his nickname was – his stupid nickname, would you believe it? Despite my protestations of innocence, Conroy proceeded to set about me in a shockingly violent manner while his pal held me immobile. He lashed me across the face with open palm. Since I was unable to defend myself I stood tall and looked him straight in the eye as he hit me again and again. I didn't shrink from his blows. While the battering was continuing, the vision of young Reilly flashed before me as he stoically accepted one hundred and ten unjust lashes to the enragement of his teacher. My lack of reaction had the same effect on Conroy and he redoubled his efforts, but he failed to get a reaction and the two of them finally swaggered off. That he didn't perceive any reaction didn't mean that there was none. The eye that I set on him became the evil eye and as he beat me I was promising myself that if I ever met those fellows out in the world later in life I would exact a revenge. "May those who love us, love us. For those who don't love us, may God turn their hearts. And if God can't turn their hearts, may He turn their ankles so we'll know them by their limping" (Old Irish Proverb).

A good memory was of finally getting home for the Christmas holidays to my family and our 'toy house'. We had been told by older students that after spending almost four months in the lofty halls and corridors of the college, we would be shocked at how tiny our house would seem. They were not pulling our legs – we were shocked. I have no recollection of that holiday in terms of activities, so I presume that I just fitted back seamlessly into the old happy routine. The only negative note was that I was only now learning of happenings in the family and the community during my absence. Had I been home I would have been in the thick of it. The sense of exclusion, which I would feel more and more on each holiday, lay heavily on me. I do have a happy memory of going over to Uncle Pee and saying "Thanks very much Pee for collecting my Ballymacad Hounds raffle prize. If you have the tenner now I could use it". "Oh! Was it yours then?" said he, laughing, "Since I was the only Peter Tuite around I thought that I must have bought a ticket and forgotten about it. I accepted the prize when the organisers insisted that it must be mine. Here you are then and congratulations!" I had bought the ticket in early September before going off to St Finian's. This incident brought home to me the truth of the saying 'Out of sight, out of mind.'

Returning to college in January was a miserable experience, but I got over it. Mullingar is one of the coldest places in Ireland, but despite this none of us ever wore an overcoat or any extra clothing. During cold spells then, I was not the only one sticking his chest out on our walks. What with cold walks and cold showers (I can remember only cold showers) and other energy sapping activities – I often walked off one football pitch after a game to play another immediately on a different pitch – we were almost coasting through our adolescence. We were not allowed to have a bath, and we speculated about the rationale for that! We were, of course, at that time, and for all our time in the college, packed with testosterone. Our sense of humour was our only way to meet that challenge as we got to know ourselves. I read recently of new research which demonstrates that cold showers actually increase testosterone. Way to go!

So, my first year in boarding school was a bit traumatic, but in the end it worked out satisfactorily in academic terms as I was promoted to the first stream for the following year. There was no lack of a sense of fun among us despite our early sadness. I remember plotting with two or three other lads who had not a note in their heads to surprise Mr Seagers, the opera music man, with the quality of our voices. When I entered for my audition he said gruffly: "Well, what are you going to sing for me?" "Daisy Sir". "Sing then". When I got as far as the second Daisy he interrupted me very rudely, saying crudely "Dood bye Daisy". He was a Belgian who spoke English badly. My co-conspirators got similar treatment and we had a good laugh.

In terms of football, having moved on from kicking a pig's bladder around the yard at home, I was now a useful enough footballer. This showed on my first summer holidays when I played for Oldcastle. During this holiday I guess that I carried on as before, helping brother Olo on the farm, wandering the countryside, especially the Loughcrew Hills, poaching trout, helping the younger children build their swimming pool dam, and refraining from the futile pursuit of rabbits. I can recall visiting Mrs Blaney, the owner of the she-goat, and I hope that I called on Mrs Reynolds, Mrs Purcell and my other old friends. I missed the company of my brother Pat who had gone off to work in Navan.

There is no lack of clarity in remembering the swim in Lough Sheelin that infected me with scabies a few days before returning to Finian's for second year in September 1949. It made all of the following year an annus horribilis. The correct treatment for scabies, in 1949 anyway, was a hot bath, a scrubbing brush, plenty of soap and the spreading of a foul smelling lotion on the scrubbed area. This treatment needed multiple applications. I will never forget the name of this evil lotion – Benzyl Benzoate Emulsion! Unfortunately, the care offered by the Matron, a nun nurse, was to hand me a bottle of the filthy stuff with instructions to apply liberally as I got into bed. The ban on taking a bath may have contributed to this poor woman's decision. In any event, once I had gotten a sniff of it there was no way that I was going to open the smelly bottle in a sixty-person dormitory. Imagine a new nickname 'Smelly'! The consequences were that for each night of September through to the end of November, I got at most a couple of hours exhausted sleep after an all-night scratching marathon!

It took my mother's intervention when she visited in early December to get proper treatment. She was shocked at my condition, a condition that must have been visible to the staff for some time, but no one asked if I was all right. I was right about the egocentricity all right! The psychological and physical damage was huge and my little world collapsed about me. For many months after this unpleasant experience the chest out, confident young lad was replaced by a sickly waif of a boy, lacking in confidence, energy and good humour. In fact I don't think that I ever fully recovered my confidence despite the confident face which I presented to the world.

The pressure put on me in class for non-performance was keenly felt as it was an unusual place for me to be in. The final humiliation was inflicted on me when Jack Lynch, our maths teacher, asked me to do theorem 29 on the board. I was so far behind that I could not do it and he sent me back to my seat (front seat now as my eyes had failed during the sleepless period) saying "Eh eh – there will be no free class tomorrow (last class of term) until Peter Tuite has done theorem 29 on the board". This meant that I had to demonstrate that the square on the hypotenuse equals the sum of the squares on the other two sides – will I ever forget it? A few minutes study in the evening enabled me to whiz through it the next day.

A sobering feature of that year was that I knew I was capable of better but I could not get myself out of the slough I was in.

With the Lough Sheelin disaster in mind I made sure not to go swimming anywhere for a couple of weeks before returning to St Finians for the commencement of my third year there. I had been reassigned to the lower stream and in class I settled in the back desk with Larry Arthur and got myself back on track. Larry was to some extent just marking time. His real interest was music, in particular the mouth organ he carried around. In later life he became a well-known entertainer in the midlands. One December day many years later when I was driving through his village my car broke down and as I was standing on the street waiting for it to be fixed I saw a young woman nearby also waiting for someone or something. I approached her and asked her if by any chance she knew Larry Arthur? She replied "I ought to, he's my father." Later on in that third year we were moved to the front desk after Larry showed his interest in Greek by reading a comic, a 'penny dreadful' Jimmy Grehan called it. Jimmy's (Caligula's) punishment was to push Larry's face down, one ear on the desktop, and to slap down on the other ear. This way he had the satisfaction of getting Larry on both cheeks with only one blow! This didn't bother Larry at all, for like most of us, he would rather a wallop than a lecture. Pain was fleeting, a lecture was a drag!

This was an 'Inter' (Intermediate Certificate) year. Having largely recovered from the trauma of the previous year, things went well and I got first stream results in my exam, much to the surprise of my previous year's teachers who had failed to notice that my poor performance was down to my evident ill health. Jimmy Grehan was the only member of staff to comment on it and to congratulate me for doing so well. With improved health my football activities became more enjoyable and the quality of life improved greatly. The year flew and before I knew it I was back helping Olo on the farm in the summer holidays.

Year four was a disaster of my own making. I lost interest in learning, did the minimum amount of homework to keep the teachers off my back and generally wasted my precious time. Dad's 'auld eejit' was alive and well! I could never account for my disinterest and my lethargy, even with hindsight.

All I can remember about fourth year is we had a flu epidemic in the college for some weeks before the Leinster Junior Championship final, which curtailed training and left a couple of our star players in bed on match day. The match was in Carlow and the opposition was Good

Council, New Ross. The game went to extra time during the course of which many of our players were suffering severely with cramps through lack of fitness and we were beaten. I didn't get the flu then, but succumbed at the end of the year and missed the summer exams.

September 1952 was the beginning of my final year in St Finian's, a year during which career decisions were going to have to be made and the Leaving Certificate Exams had to be faced. Shortly after returning there I discovered an old library adjoining the study hall. While rooting around in it I came across bound copies of Sir Walter Scott's Waverley Novels. All my good resolutions about study went out the window at that very moment. One of the books was quickly transferred to my desk and from then until December I read a good number of them during the three evening hours allocated to study. I probably gave only a half hour each evening to homework. It just was not sensible to neglect study of Leaving Cert subjects, for obvious reasons. Yet I have never regretted devoting that precious time to the reading of Scott's romantic historical tales. There was a theme of idealism running through most, if not all, of these novels which appealed strongly to me. In terms of the Leaving Cert, Scott was not good; in terms of a major contribution to my ability to write good English and to being idealistic myself in my approach to a cynical world, Scott was hugely influential. He was worth the loss of about three honours in the Leaving.

On the football front, that year was major. We had a fine team, strong in every position and we swept all before us in winning the 1953 Leinster title. Because of a puritanical Bishop in Longford, there was no All Ireland Colleges competition that year. We would have fancied our chances, as seven or eight of our team were on the Leinster team that won the Interprovincial Championship. The Bishop had banned Sunday football and nobody had what it took to put him in his place.

On the handball front it was also a good year. Jim Ryan was Prefect that year and as such he was free to move around at will. He could therefore leave the refectory before anyone else and stroll down to book a handball alley. It wasn't fair, but weren't we all egocentrics? By the end of the year he and I were the best handballers in the school. He beat me in the final of the singles and in the doubles he and Kieran Dunican, I think, beat Tom McDonnell and myself. Jim was not as mobile as I but he had a deadly butt (killing the ball at the butt of the wall). He was also more ruthless than me as he invaded his less accomplished partner's territory frequently if his partner was struggling.

Sometime during the year I had decided that I was going to try my vocation to the priesthood. When I told Gisty Gilsenan from Dromone what I was contemplating doing he exclaimed "Jaysus, what will you do if you get a horn"? I can't remember what I said in reply. I suppose I might have joked "What's that"? I was unsure that I had a vocation, but no harm could be done by giving it a try. The fact that there weren't many career opportunities out there would have influenced that decision. I was not thinking clearly at all during this time. An example of poor decision making was that I quit the Greek exam after forty five minutes and fell short of an honour by two marks. It was the last exam and I could not get out of there quickly enough. I also bumped into a strongly disapproving Larry Fagan outside the door and he sent me away with a flea in my ear. Another doubtful decision was to accompany Seamus Mc Phillips and Maurice Creegan on a forbidden trip to the lake. The two lads had sourced a bottle of cider somewhere and by the time we reached the lake they were merry. We had a quick swim and made our way back stealthily and safely to the college grounds. Had we been caught it would have been immediate expulsion.

Back in Ballinvalley I enjoyed my freedom and engaged in all the usual pursuits with gusto. I went on pilgrimage with Dad and some of his friends to Lough Derg. I think Hugh Reilly, Pee Kimmins and Tommy Ashe were part of the group. You stayed for two nights. The first night you walked around in your bare feet all night inside the church doing the Stations or saying the rosary, finishing with six o'clock mass in the morning. On all the three visits that I made there I missed the sermon at this mass as I fell asleep in a kneeling position on a stairway. During the next day there were 'Stations' on and off during the day with long rest periods. The stations consisted of barefoot walking from rock to rock, reciting the rosary or other prayers. My Dad and his friends enjoyed themselves during the rest periods and there was much laughter and banter among them. You were starved of sleep and food there, your only food intake consisting of dry toast and black tea. I still drink my tea black!

Services continued into late evening on the second day, but you finally got to bed. Boy, was that a great sleep! The following morning the boat pulled in and we headed back to the mainland and the Pettigo train to Clones where we had left the truck. We had to continue fasting until midnight at which time we tucked into a big fry. The following day I togged out for Oldcastle and I was like a salmon, leaping for balls and playing out of my skin. A bit of fasting does the body and the mind no harm! I went on this pilgrimage twice more in the following years and each time I had a match on my return with the same result.

DALGAN

The first day in St Columban's, Dalgan Park in September 1953, was a civilized affair with the older students gathering around and making us welcome. St Finian's footballers had been guests at Dalgan during the year and we had had a ding-dong battle with their team which included a few county players. The names of Des Maguire (Cavan and Oldcastle), Peter Tierney (Galway) and Peter Conlon (Louth) spring to mind. The lads we had met on the footballing visit were all there – we were almost smothered in bonhomie.

The first month was spent familiarising ourselves with the place and the people (about two hundred in all, thirty-one of these being first years). We, the Probos as new entrants were called because the first year was a probation year, were also being prepared for the big October event – a thirty days retreat following the dictats of St Ignatius of Loyola. The thirty days would be spent in silence except on the three break days. The first break came after ten days, the second after eighteen and the third after twenty four (I think). Cynics might call it a brainwashing exercise, it probably was all of that, but it was very simply an attempt to help us to find out who we really were, where we wanted to go and how we were going to get there.

For all of us it was a difficult challenge, for some it was traumatic, and for one or two, impossible. One lad went off his head and was sent home, and one or two others quit. The lads who had come from places like St Finian's managed quite well as they were partly broken in already, but poor fellows who had been dayboys and had never left their family circles went through hell. As for me, I was toughing it out well in the first week until one day on one of my long walks a car pulled up with a squeal of brakes and the occupants waited for me in the car. It was Michael Heery and his family. In the back seat was his daughter Detta, a Holy Faith Convent student I had exchanged romantic letters with during my fourth year in Finian's. I didn't know where to look, and stupidly I felt constrained to limit talking because of the no talking rule. We did exchange a few words, I declined a lift and they motored on out of sight. Why didn't I just jump into the seat beside Detta and disappear over the horizon? Towards the tail-end of the ten days my mind was defunct and my body was going mad.

I was back in equilibrium for the remainder of the retreat and afterwards I immersed myself in football the three kinds: GAA, soccer and rugby. I played basketball and rackets in between and when I had free time I got a scythe and in the company of Pat Egan set about maintaining the grounds. The Probos also had the weekly task of waxing and polishing the parquet floors, corridors, class halls and other rooms on the ground floor, and the corridors on the second and third floors. There were four one-hundred-yard-long corridors with all the rooms off (on the ground floor) so it was not a token job. We were not allowed home for Christmas or Easter that year and various outside activities were encouraged. The biggest event at Christmas was a cross country race. After a few trial runs the race itself was held and the whole class set off at a signal from Tom Caffrey. Jim MacDonnell romped home a hundred yards ahead of Pat O'Sullivan and myself. Pat and I were fitter even than Jim but our body shapes were not quite right for long distance running. Jim played centerfield for Cavan later on and left for a career in teaching. The last I heard of him he was Principal of St Pat's in Cavan.

At Easter the main activity was walking. There were shortish walks to Bective across the fields (in the course of which we passed close to Mary Lavin's house and sometimes engaged her and, I think, her young daughter in conversation). The longer walks were to Slane, a thirty kilometres round trip and to Mellifont Abbey, about fifty kilometres. In between was Newgrange and its ancient monuments. We used to walk across the Boyne at the ramparts to get to the main Cairn. I never heard of anyone falling into the river, surprisingly. Our biggest problem until we got hardened to it was being 'stymied' – blisters in the groin area!

The sporting year ended with a flourish with a daylong sports fest. Everyone got involved in a light-hearted manner, either as organisers or competitors. I can't remember all the events, but I do remember that I won the shot put and the high jump, an unusual combination. I also came in second in a couple of other events, one of them being the egg and spoon race! But best of all, Pat O'Sullivan and I won the three-legged race. This was enough to swing the top athlete 'award' my way. Before the award was confirmed there was a good-humoured objection from the loser on the basis that the three-legged race should not count since it was just a fun thing that was not athletics. Owen O'Leary, a lovely young man and the chief organiser, sidled up to me apologetically to tell me that they would find it difficult to resist the objection. I parried with persuasive arguments that the three-legged race was the most important event in the program. There was not a school sports day in the country that did not have it as a key event, not only for the children, but also for the supporting parents. Were we not a school and were we not all children of God? A prolonged discussion ensued in which bystanders participated. It was extremely jocular and when Owen declared in my favour there was humorous applause.

Home we went then for the long summer holidays with its usual round of farm work, swimming, football and walkabouts. I had played for Oldcastle teams on and off since I was about twelve, largely with the same group of lads but with important players being lost every year to emigration. I was privileged to be involved for so long with such a great group of lads. At this time the chairman was Paddy Kearney, a brother of Margo, Eithne Lynch's friend. Paddy's father was a well-known taxi man whose biggest claim to fame was that he always picked up Lord Longford from Oldcastle train station and delivered him to his estate about ten miles away near Castlepollard. Paddy was passionate about the football and his team but because of the emigration drain and our lack of success on the field, there was pressure to consider an amalgamation of the three clubs in the parish. In order to be seen to be giving serious consideration to this, Paddy arranged a meeting with Michael Tuite of Knockbrack and his committee in charge of the Millbrook team. Moylough would be next if we could get a good result from this meeting. We started off with a concession – we agreed to meet in Michael's house in Knockbrack. Paddy was particularly anxious that I should attend and I went along willingly. The meeting started off well and progress was made until we got down to the nitty-gritty of who was going to be in control. To my dismay I then realised that Paddy was interested only in a takeover, not an amalgamation. The meeting broke up. I had gone there in good faith with an open mind. Paddy had me there in my sober dark seminarian suit because my presence would inspire trust. I felt a bit used. I felt sorry for Michael Tuite who was just as passionate about his football as Paddy. That was exactly sixty years ago in 1954. The amalgamation never happened and the team still fails to perform on the field. I have no doubt that the lads enjoy their football anyway, but I can't help feeling that they would get much more satisfaction and fun out of it if they could play and succeed at a higher level.

During our first year in Dalgan we attended classes as a normal routine. We had a few subjects, the most important of which were English, Latin (many of our textbooks in the following year and thereafter were in Latin), Scripture and spirituality. The following two years were devoted to studies in philosophy – metaphysics and logic were two important ones. We also studied the ancient Greek philosophers – Plato, Socrates, Aristotle and some others as well as some of the modern philosophers. Music, elocution, English and French were among the lighter subjects. The music-cum-French teacher, Bill Halliday, firmly believed that everybody could sing, even me. (I had told him about being removed from the singing class in National school). During these two years I did a modest amount of study and played a lot of games. I also took up study of the French language seriously after discovering a gramophone player and some Assimil records in one of the reading rooms. A couple of other lads joined me and we practised our atrocious French as we walked around the grounds in our free time.

The years flew and in the summer of 1956 the college arranged for Seamus Farrelly and me to go to France for five weeks to improve our French. We were to go to Nevers, a town some sixty miles south of Paris to stay initially in a seminary there and then join a group of about sixty children with their minders in Brittany for three weeks. The group was to be called 'Les Ecureuils du Nivernais' (The Squirrels of Nivernais). We were also booked into a hotel in Paris for three nights on the way so that we could absorb some of the culture. Our first exposure to the 'culture' as we exited our hotel in Rue Lafayette was to be approached by two young ladies who asked in the sweetest voices "Monsieur Veut-il?" When we realised what was on offer we declined politely and scurried down the street. We walked Paris for the two days visiting all the usual places, the churches: Notre Dame, Montmartre, and the Madeleine, and one or two museums. Then the money ran out after we hired a row-boat at the lake in Bois de Boulogne. It was not that we were extravagant, it was just that Paris was an extremely expensive place. We had been living on cheese-filled French rolls and tasty chicory coffee, and after our first coke cost us more than twice the Irish price we drank water. We contacted the college in some embarrassment and a few pounds were cabled to us. That was all we had for the remainder of our visit as everything was paid for except the cost of an omnibus from deep in Brittany to St Malo where we were to catch the boat for the first stage of our trip home.

From Paris we caught a train to Nevers and made our way to our seminary lodgings. We were in Nevers because some of the Columbans knew the local bishop whose name was O'Flynn. We visited him and found him to be a lovely man. He said he envied the Irish Church with its packed churches and exceptionally good resources. He had been the Parish Priest of the Madeleine, one of the wealthiest parishes in Paris, but his diocese in the Department of Nivernais was one of the poorest in both numbers of the faithful and in money. He himself was a descendant of one of the Wild Geese. His personal assistant was a fascinating character. She was a heroine of the disastrous defeat at Dien Bien Phu in 1954 having been a nurse there. Her name was Geneviève de Galard and I remembered her name dominating the media at the time as 'The Angel of Dien Bien Phu'. Unfortunately she was ill when we visited and we did not get a chance to talk to her.

We also got a special personal tour of the local Chateau. This was arranged by a man from Cork University called McCarthy who spent his summers in the area and had formed a friendship with the Seigneur. He had his nine-year-old son with him. The son took us in hand to show us the ropes and to rescue us when our faltering French failed us. He was an impressive young boy. Back in the seminary, pretty well deserted in this holiday season, I sat out in the beautiful garden to admire it and listen to the crickets, a new experience for me – we didn't get those fellows in Ballinvalley! I was joined after a while by a little priest who engaged me in conversation. It was a struggle as I was not sufficiently fluent in French at that stage and he suggested that we should try a little Latin. To my surprise that worked very well, for though many of our textbooks were in Latin, we had never attempted to use it outside of the classroom. For a while after that I was tempted to add Latin to the list of languages I spoke! We managed to have a couple of swims in the Loire before we headed off for Brittany. It was a little scary as we had been told that there was quite a lot of dangerous quicksand along the river so we kept very close to some locals for safety. There was, of course, the obligatory visit to pray by the perfectly preserved body of St Bernadette.

Before the trip to Brittany we got a briefing from the young Dutch priest who was organising and leading the 'Colonie de Vacance' in Brittany. It was, disappointingly, a very short briefing – not much more than details of the train we were to take and our destination. After an unexpected day-long journey, much of it standing in the corridor of a packed train, we arrived in Brest around midnight. We still had a twenty kilometre journey into the wilds of Brittany ahead of us, and to our dismay there was no public transport at that time of night. It was not the inconvenience that dismayed us but the cost in relation to the few francs in our pockets. We sought out a taxi service and managed to agree a price that would leave us just enough to get to St Malo at the end of the holiday. Whew! We could imagine the reaction if the college got another begging cable from us! Anyway, we arrived bedraggled and weary at Grouanec-en-Plouguerneau and tumbled straight into bed in a schoolroom which had been converted into a dormitory for the summer. It was an excellent use of idle facilities during holiday time and I believe the practice was widespread in France.

The following morning, having been awakened by the clamp-clamp of sabots on the road outside as the womenfolk went off to work in the fields, we discovered that our group was composed of the priest, a cook, six moniteurs, including Seamus and me, and sixty boys aged from about seven to fifteen. Our inclusion in the moniteurs slot was a bit of a joke initially, due to our struggle for fluency in the language. I discovered after a few days of getting my ears attuned that some of the precocious smaller boys who had been gathering in a group near me for a couple of days with much talk and laughter, were telling extremely dirty jokes, knowing that I hadn't an idea of what they were up to. Of course when I laughed with them they rolled about the place with mirth. I soon sorted them out when I copped on.

Our cook was brilliant. The first evening we sat down to a dinner of the most delicious potato soup, soaking in Marshall Plan butter. (We had a supply of big sealed cans of this American butter which had been poured into war-torn Europe with other foodstuffs for a few years after the war to help get the place on its feet again). I had two generous helpings and was just waiting for the 'Grace after meals' when a trolley rumbled in with more heaped dishes of food. By the end of that course I was pretty full and I awaited the 'Grace' again. Lo and behold, the door slapped open again and there were more big dishes. After another repeat of this I finally gave up, excused myself from the table and waddled off. St Finian's did not prepare me for five courses! Her food was wonderful and she gave the same performance every night of our stay.

We had a brilliant time. It was great fun organising activities for the boys and joining in. We interrupted our games one day to pick potatoes for a local farmer in order to raise funds for an excursion into Brest. A lot of the potatoes seemed to take on wings and to land with force on my body – little brats! We headed out on the excursion the following day by a circuitous route in order to enjoy the impressive scenery and to visit France's great warship, the Richelieu. She was built in Brest in 1935 and tied up there in 1956. She had an interesting history, having fought off the British navy when they attacked Dakar, then controlled by the Vichy regime. Later, in 1943, she had joined the British fleet for the remainder of the war. Seamus and I, as foreigners, were barred from boarding and we had to sit out the visit on the dock. Quel dommage that we could not have been temporary Frenchmen!

Les Ecureuils du Nivernais in Brest July 1956

After a week or ten days listening to the children with their limited and repetitive language, and having long chats in the evenings with the adults, we were not only understanding the language and speaking it fluently if sometimes incorrectly, we were thinking in the language. This was a great breakthrough for us and we had already achieved the primary objective of our trip. Seamus and I had agreed before our travels that once we got on the boat we would speak only French to each other. We were faithful to this arrangement throughout, but there were times when I woefully missed hearing my own language. One day we all visited a famous lighthouse on a rugged part of the coast in the vicinity. While there I heard English being spoken by a young honeymoon couple. I quickly attached myself to them – the joy of being able to hear and speak my own language! They were in love and at that wonderful time in their lives they loved everyone, so they not only tolerated my hanging around, they encouraged me and seemed to enjoy my company as much as I enjoyed theirs.

The holiday came to an end too quickly. The boys went back to their homes in great good humour and the picture of health. Seamus and I took an omnibus bound for St Malo and the ferry. The 'omni' part of that word should have alerted us Latin scholars to its nature – a bus that goes everywhere before it arrives! Up and down byways we went all day, stopping for everyone, anywhere. The driver, a feisty little man fought with anyone who crossed him. On narrow roads he bullied much bigger men into backing up and letting him pass if he thought the road could not take a bus and a car at the same time. He rolled down the window and yelled at any driver who dared blow his horn in the rear. He was nice to elderly women and young children, but he expected everyone else to look out for themselves. We learnt some new words from him that we would not use in everyday conversation! No geese, turkeys or hens came aboard, but we expected that at every stop. In addition we got a detailed tour of some lovely, sometimes remote, countryside. However, we had a ferry to catch and we had anxious moments towards the end in case we missed it. (We weren't too sure that we had enough funds to make alternative arrangements). We made it by a hairsbreadth.

We boarded and made directly to the restaurant as we had not eaten all day. We gulped down a big fry but as soon as the ship hit the open sea we staggered to the side and dumped it overboard! It was a bad night. The ship rocked and heaved in the huge waves and the wind whistled in the rigging, but we made land eventually in a SE English port the name of which I can't recall. We disembarked, white faced, staggered to the train, and the long journey to Holyhead began. Not a pleasant journey, especially the Euston to Holyhead packed train, and the cattle boat from there to Dun Laoghaire. We were glad at last to get home and to have a couple of weeks with our families before returning to Dalgan for our fourth, and my final year. Seamus went on to ordination but he quit after a few years and he died young in America.

During the summer, doubts about my vocation became stronger and I returned to Dalgan in September in an uncertain frame of mind. During the Christmas holidays I decided that I should abandon further thoughts of the priesthood, so off I went then to tell Fr Brennan that I was leaving. He did not put any pressure on me to reconsider, but he did ask me if the refusal of the college to allow me out to play for Oldcastle in the recent county final had a bearing on my decision. I disabused him of that notion by stating that the matter in hand was much more important than a game of football. He gave me his blessing and before I departed we had a brief discussion on the options, perhaps I should say non-options, available career wise. Fr Brennan was a very well-liked man. He once mounted the pulpit, when there was a full gathering of the students, to comment on a weeklong retreat that a 'hell and damnation' preacher had given to us during the previous week. He said "I would like to reaffirm to you all that you are not a bunch of criminals, you are seminarians. I suggest that you forget everything that that man said to you during the past week." We applauded him in our hearts.

Dalgan was good for me. I was lucky to have had the privilege of spending three and a half years there, surrounded by ordinary lads from all over Ireland. With few exceptions they were strongly idealistic, with a total absence of egocentricity. They were all on the one wavelength, consideration for others was the norm and they all wanted to make a difference.

EMIGRATION

In early January 1957, shortly after I had left Dalgan, I was walking in O'Connell Street in Dublin when I came across a group of Frenchmen. They were in a huddle on the pavement having a voluble discussion. It turned out that they were Bretons and they were looking for a bistro. With my now fluent French I was anxious to help and I took them to a 'character' pub in the absence of such a thing as a bistro in Dublin. They were fishermen whose boat was tied up in the docks while they were awaiting the abatement of the very stormy weather we were experiencing at that time. After the pub I went with them to their boat and before I left them I was invited to go with them to Brittany where they would find me a beautiful girl and I could settle down there! The captain was an ex-seminarian like myself and I was tempted. The memory of the stormy crossing of the Channel the previous August and the fact that I did not have my passport with me prevented me from taking on the adventure and a totally unexpected new direction in life.

A few days later my Uncle Johnny accompanied me out to Dun Laoghaire and waved me on to the ferry to Holyhead. It was the last time I saw him, as he died a few months later. A recent article in the Irish Times made an argument that Irish emigrants did not go to America, they went to relatives or friends, the implication being that that was all right then. If I had read that while sailing into the stormy night in that miserable January I would have put a match to it with rage in my heart. I was driven out of an Ireland run by an uncaring elite of civil servants and politicians who did nothing, absolutely nothing, to create opportunities for anybody except themselves. The two men who, too late for me, finally bestirred themselves to do something to plug the brain drain, Whittaker and Lemass, deserve to live in the memories of the tens of thousands of young Irishmen and women who could stay at home in the sixties and seventies as a result of their efforts. It was to a foreign country that I was going, not to visit relatives even though some of them were there. I had no illusions about a nice family reunion – I was going to be living among and working with strangers who generally had no regard for the Irish. What a change it was going to be from life in a caring community. Sure, I was met at Euston station by my sister Dilly and she arranged temporary accommodation for me with her landlady. (A good kind woman who went to great trouble to prepare a special breakfast for me on my first day – a soft egg on a kipper. Neither the egg nor the kipper would figure on a list of my favourite foods, but what could I do but eat them with appreciative comments). Once I had arranged alternative accommodation I was on my own, I had to forage for myself.

My first experience was an eye opener. When looking for accommodation, I was amused and sad at the same time to read notices on doors of residences which had advertised for tenants. "No coloured, no Irish, no dogs". At least we were only the second most unpopular! Sometimes the dogs were not included. These notices were not a myth as claimed by a recent contributor to the Irish Times. I saw it with my own eyes on doors all over London. If I had not been amused I would probably have been enraged, but I understood that many of the landladies behind those doors were possibly women widowed by the war who read scurrilous stuff about Africans, West Indians and Irish in the gutter press. It was fear that spawned this racism, not badness. At the same time I was well aware that there was a lot of drinking and fighting among far too many Irish. The 'Paddy Wagon' got its name for a good reason. This behaviour was reported by the tabloids without any attempt ever to give credit to the majority of Irish immigrants who went quietly and efficiently about their business in all walks of life.

Anyway, I got digs in a small room in Acton, West London, near Ealing. For the first couple of weeks I applied for jobs in banks, insurance companies and in one case in some desperation for a job in Africa. I got no reply and as money was running out I decided that I needed to lower my sights and to take any old job that would put food on the table for the time being. Down I went to the London Transport medical reception centre where they medically examined applicants before the actual job interview. My name was called, I approached the doctor and before I got within four metres of her she yelled at me "Get out of here – didn't I tell you never to come here again". And I thought I was unique!!

So then there was British Rail, but before I tried them I happened to meet Gerry Daly, chairman of St Mary's football club and of London GAA. I briefed him on my situation and my background and out of the blue he said I should go to see a friend of his who was in the wine importing business. He had been looking for a French speaker who would be capable in time of doing all the travelling to the vineyards, selecting the wines and purchasing them. Wow! This was it, the breakthrough! I did not delay in arranging an appointment, we liked each other and I got the job as his personal assistant. There was a catch, however. I must start from the bottom for a month or two to familiarise myself with all the detail. This entailed initially sharing the work with about a half dozen youngsters doing paperwork. The next bit is something I am embarrassed and disappointed about. I was so bad at what I was doing that towards the end the youngsters were sniggering behind my back: I could not handle the figures. Go on, admit it – I couldn't add. A couple of months later I could run my finger up two rows of figures (shillings and pence) and come up with a speedy and correct answer, but now I was useless. Finally, after three weeks I suggested to my boss that the situation wasn't doing either him or me any good and we agreed that I should depart. That was a bitter disappointment – no – a humiliation for me. I knew that I wasn't stupid so instead of slinking into the undergrowth to lick my wounds, I practised adding row upon row of figures in my idle moments until I mastered it.

It was off to British Rail then! I became a ticket clerk at Willesden Junction, a combined railway and underground station in NW London. On my first day on the job, which was within walking distance, I had to feel my way along a fence to get there. The smog was so dense that visibility was no more than a metre. It was a choking, thick smog which left a black residue in my nose and throat. I worked there for a few months, getting diddled once by a few Irish workers passing through on a Friday night. They put their tool boxes in store and then early on Monday morning turned up with no money for the storage fee. With promises of payment the following Friday ringing in my ears I released the tool boxes, never saw them again, and was obliged to make the payments out of my own pocket.

It seems that Fate was taking a hand and that all previous activities and events were leading to one thing – an encounter with May Quinn, my future wife, mother of my nine children and grandmother to twenty-five grandchildren, great grandmother to two, so far. I was on an evening shift at the ticket office when a fellow approached with a shadowy figure behind him. He was intending to go to Ireland later on in the summer and he was wondering how to get to where he was going? An Irishman wanting to know how to get to Ireland? May and I have joked about it many times, I claiming it was a setup to enable the fellow, Edward, to get rid of his sister, she claiming that she didn't like the look of me and that's why she concealed herself behind him. Anyway, she eventually showed her face, smiling to dazzle, and that was that.

May had just arrived in London from a convent in Rome where she was a postulant, and I had come from a seminary in Ireland. Neither of us had the faintest idea of how to manage dealing with a non-family member of the opposite sex. As we were walking out on our first date I offered my arm saying, "Why don't you take the weight off your bones?" She stepped briskly away from me, the expression on her face indicating that I was very 'forward'. We went to the cinema where we laughed boisterously at 'Lucky Jim' and 'Monsieur Hulot's Holiday'. I saw Lucky Jim years later and it was the unfunniest drivel! I bought a bag of sweets for May and she later claimed that I ate them all myself!

During the course of the following year we saw a lot of London in our leisure hours. We walked all the parks – Hyde Park, Regents Park, Hampstead Heath, Kew Gardens, the Zoo and the other 'zoo' – Hyde Park or Speakers' Corner. We also went dancing in the Galtymore in Cricklewood, having first attended dance classes in the Victor Sylvester Studio on Kilburn High Road. I had left British Rail and I was working in a lowly job with Colgate Palmolive. My boss there was an elderly man called Conner, from O'Connor which he had changed so that he would not be recognised as Irish. It wasn't good to be Irish in the England of his young days. Things were getting serious with May, and I decided that I had better find a better job that would offer me a career so I began to apply to all the usual suspects again. Luckily Barclays Bank took me on as a clerk in their Chief Foreign branch. It was ironic that I lost the job I really liked because I couldn't add, and now, after shining at figures in their training school, I had been given this posting because I was outstanding at figures!

May & Peter in The Galtymore, Cricklewood, 1958

At Barclays Bank Training School 1958

Chief Foreign branch was huge. It serviced all Barclays' branches in the Midlands and south-east England. Many of the staff were ex RAF, some of them war heroes. They had seen it all and the management had a difficult job trying to manage them. They were good efficient workers, but they were also free spirits. I and the many Irish working in the branch got on exceptionally well with them. Among the Irish girls there was a big handsome lass from Mayo. One day a smallish fellow pinched her bottom as she leaned over a copying machine. She swung round and with a mighty wallop left him sitting on the floor several paces away. I witnessed this as did a few of the free spirits, and they loved her for it! In my area we had six or seven Barclay's pensioners working part-time for the summer which was our busy time. They handled some routine work, which freed me up to do all the figures. They were lovely men. After I had been there a year, and presumably after he had disabused himself of the notion that the Irish were exactly as frequently described in Punch, one of the more retiring men sidled up to me and confessed with some trepidation that he had been a Black and Tan! They all worked hard without missing any opportunity to be merry, tell jokes and pull each other's legs. One of them told me privately about a female staff member who had just got engaged and had had an engagement party. He asked her how she enjoyed it, she responded "Cor! It didn't half hurt". I hadn't known that that was how they got engaged!

There were only two or three Irish men in the branch and I formed a friendship with Mike Healy, an ex-Newbridge College lad who had been there for a while. Mike was playing with the third reserve team in London Irish Rugby Club and he persuaded me to join up. The team was captained by George Morrison from the North. George was not a great player but he was an inspirational leader and we all loved playing under his command. He was a bit unorthodox. For example if we were flagging in a game he would shout "A pint to the next fellow to score a try", with the result that we were fighting each other for the ball. The teams in London Irish were put together in such a way that their composition was as near as possible to 50-50 Irish and Northern Irish with possibly one or two Australians thrown in. There was never ever any trouble arising from our different perceptions of things 'up there'. We did well in all our games and one other teammate and I were promoted to the second team but we were happy where we were and refused to go. I had a few injuries while playing for London Irish, the most serious of which was a concussion so severe that I lost my sight for about twelve hours. That was scary. Poor George jumped off Westminster Bridge a few years later.

Sometime in 1960 I left London Irish to join the bank's rugby club. My first game was against Woodford and I was playing for the reserves. I hasten to say for reasons that will quickly become clear that the standard in bank rugby would not be quite at the level of London Irish. When entering the ground I noticed an old man on the sideline. He was shrunken with age and infirmity but he was still instantly recognisable as Sir Winston Churchill. Woodford had been his constituency. As a young boy during the war I had been impressed by Churchill's barnstorming speeches. One did not have to be an adult to appreciate the delivery, the defiance, the use of language. The neighbours used to gather in our house and outside the open window to hear the news of the war, especially at times when bad news was arriving from the Allied side. There was no doubt that we were all afraid of a German victory. We also were aware of the spat between Churchill and DeValera. Churchill didn't make himself too popular with the Irish.

The game began and it quickly became clear that we were totally outclassed. I was playing full back – the last man standing. The opposition was coming down on me in swarms – I tackled right, I tackled left, I tackled high and I tackled low with an occasional Gaelic shoulder thrown in, and still they kept coming. Occasionally I was able to wrestle the ball from an opponent and make some little runs of my own. I was in a fight that I was enjoying hugely, but in the end they breached the line and we were comprehensively beaten. After the game the coach entered the dressing room, stood on the bench, sought silence and said "You will all have noticed our distinguished guest, Sir Winston Churchill on the sideline. Well Sir Winston has asked me to congratulate, and here I quote, "The young Irishman for a magnificent performance". I think that it was an impressive performance by him that he, who had ruled an empire and whose peers had been the most powerful men on earth, took the trouble to send a nice message to a young man, and an Irishman to boot.

Barclays Bank Rugby Club 1ˢᵗ XV 1962-1963: J.W. Dodds (Chairman), R. McBride, D. Belsham, D. Price, R.J. Brett, K. Main; P. Tuite, V.F. Long, G. Boulter, B.R. Robinson (Captain), J.G. Robinson (Hon. Secretary), D. Hooper, C.J. Parker; P. Brown, M.F. O'Reilly, L. Martin

Jottings of a Country Boy

I played for Barclay's first team until we moved to Nottingham in 1963 and I must have been playing well enough as I was also on the United Banks' panel. The captain of the first team, Bev Robinson, was a lovely fellow whom I had great regard for as both a man and a leader. His brother John also played for the team. Many years later I got a surprise visit from John in my office in Cork. I was delighted to see him and enquired what he was doing there. He then admitted that he was a Corkman (of the Anglo variety) and he was going down to West Cork to visit his mother. I never got an inkling of their origins during three years of sharing battles on the rugby field.

My poor mother died in August 1958 after a long period of ill health. My boss was reluctant to let me off for the funeral — it appears that some of his staff in the past had got leave for non-existent funerals and he was not going to be caught again. It was sad that at a time when my mother should have been expecting to look forward to enjoying her numerous grandchildren (fifty in the end) she was departing this life at the young age of fifty three.

In December 1958 May and I got engaged. I must have proposed — May tells me I said "Would you ever think of marrying a fellow like me"? We went up to Our Lady of Sorrows just off the Harrow Road and got the little Irish priest there to bless us and our second hand engagement ring. The poor man killed himself a year later — there appeared to be a lot of these tragic happenings. Another colleague whom I was very fond of did the same. She was in her late fifties. She was past her best in looks and efficiency and she was not getting any respect from some of her colleagues. One Friday afternoon she came to me in a troubled frame of mind, asked me to pray for her and went home to put her head in the gas oven. I was too callow a youth to recognise that I should have invited her out for a cup of tea and a chat at the very least.

During nineteen fifty-eight and fifty-nine May and I did a lot of overtime in our respective banks. There were many new share issues being handled by all the banks and I worked in a nearby branch, sometimes five nights each week until late. May was doing the same with her employer, Lloyds bank. We could earn up to thirty pounds each on a good week. Our weekly salaries were only about ten or eleven pounds. After a while we had to restrict our overtime a bit, partly out of regard for our health. New Issues were new shares being issued by large companies who exchanged shares in the company for money or other consideration. There was an amazing amount of paperwork involved.

One Saturday night there was a poker game in our basement flat in Paddington which went on all night. Joe Flynn and his friend Mick Ryan were there, as were John and Liam Kelly and Patsy McTeague, my flatmates. I was not a great poker player and I lost every penny of overtime I had earned that week – twenty eight pounds. I never played poker for money again. I shared that basement flat with the Kelly brothers (Liam had been in my class in Dalgan) and Patsy McTeague for a couple of years. We did our own cooking – Liam did meats and vegetables, John did desserts, I did soda bread and Patsy commented from the sidelines!

May and I married on October third 1959, two years after we had met. At this time my flat was only seven minutes' walk to the flat that May was sharing with her mother and brother Edward. I should have mentioned that May's mother and all eight of May's siblings lived in London and at one stage eight of my ten siblings also lived there. The scale of the problems in Ireland that resulted in whole families being forced to seek work abroad was shocking to everybody but the elite back there who did nothing about it. After returning from honeymoon in Bognor Regis we moved into a flat in NW3 and lived happily there until our landlady discovered May was pregnant and gave us notice to quit. She was Belgian, like our 'Dood bye Daisy' music man in St Finian's. It's an ill wind... and we were given an eight-roomed flat in West Kensington by my employers at a nominal rent of twenty-nine shillings a week.

Eamon was born in August 1960 and we all moved into our spacious accommodation. Mary was born in September 1961 in that flat and we enjoyed living in the area. When Willie came to London he lived with us there until we moved – we could have accommodated half the tribe! The bank did not like to have vacant floors above the branch and all such accommodation became a perk for young couples such as ourselves.

Jottings of a Country Boy

In 1962 we bought a house in Eltham, close to Sidcup where my brother Eddie lived. We lived there for only eighteen months and during our first summer there I took on a navvying job for my two-week annual holidays. The job involved ripping up pathways in a suburban estate on the outskirts of London and laying replacements. On the first morning I was picked up at seven o'clock at Eltham Well Hall station for a fifty-minute journey in the back of a truck. On reaching the site I was handed a pick, shown a pathway to rip up and invited to go to work. At twelve o'clock when the call for lunchbreak came I slid down wearily on the side of the road almost too tired to open up my packet of sandwiches. I had thought that I was fit, but a fit man does not get cramps in his pectorals – that's what I had! It was my own fault entirely, as I was aware that all the other fellows knew that I was a bank clerk and that I would not be able to pull my weight. I therefore entered into a pseudo competition with them in order to gain a little respect. I'm not too sure of the respect, but I did have large welts on my hands and the rest of that day was not pleasant, nor were the following two days, but I stuck stubbornly at it through the pain. From day four on I was ok and the following days hardened me up again, although I have to confess that when I was dropped off each day in Eltham I had to drag myself wearily up the hill to the house. I kept a curious eye on the other fellows as I was interested in establishing how they could possibly spend their lives doing what they were doing.

There was one fairly elderly man there and I had noticed how he carried on all day picking or shovelling at an unhurried but effective pace. When I asked him how he could have done this work all his life his response was: "Well Peter, I'm just happy to have a job." All of them worked hard but they were able to ease the burden with an abundance of wit and laughter. I was very impressed with them, as were one or two of the householders who came out at the end of the job with tips and praise. I earned £30 for that fortnight. When I arrived home on the final day there was a new settee in the living room which May and her mother had bought that day for the same sum on extended credit at five shillings a week. It took me a while to work myself up to sitting in that piece of furniture!

During most of my days in London I played Gaelic football. When I lived in Acton I used to travel to south-east London to play with The Harps which had been put together by Fr Seamus Heatherton. He was from Munterconnaught and he had been a senior in St Finian's when I started in 1948. When I moved from Acton to Kilburn I joined St Mary's which was attached to Quex Road church. This church, run by the Irish Oblates, had regular attendances at Sunday masses in excess of five thousand. Harps was a junior team, (we got beaten in the final of the London championship before I left to join St Mary's) and Mary's was senior. In my last game in London we got beaten in the final again, but this time amid some controversy. During the game, a bruising encounter, the referee gave a penalty to the opposition that was not a penalty and refused to give a clear penalty to us. Threats must have been issued because about three minutes before full time, at which stage we were losing by a point, the referee sidled over to the gate of the fenced off pitch, blew the whistle and made a run for it. The officials slammed and locked the gate behind him just in time as thirteen of the team chased after him, clambering on the fence but fortunately failing to cross it. The other two members of the team, Sean Vesey from Longford and myself, could only look on with amazed amusement. We heard that the referee was discovered cowering in a neighbouring tennis court at ten o'clock that night.

Things were going only ok on the work front. I was working hard and doing a good job. Strickland, my old boss, had retired and my new boss, Bertie Brent, a Methodist lay preacher, was xenophobic. He was not good for poor Paddy's prospects of advancement. I mentioned to him once that John Brown, an Englishman, had just joined London Irish and he exploded "The bastard", splattering me with saliva. When I sought advancement I was told that if I had done the bank exams it might make a difference. When I did them I was told there were no guarantees. So when I was offered a position as a founding member of a new foreign branch in Nottingham I accepted with alacrity. We sold our Eltham house and bought a newly built one in Radcliffe-on-Trent, a few miles outside Nottingham, again with a low-rate bank loan. Even though the bank paid for removal, for some reason I was persuaded by Mike Healy to buy an old van which would be useful for removal of some odds and ends of our possessions. The van cost fifteen pounds (that was too much for it), and we loaded it up inside and out. There was hardly any steering and we meandered, I use the word advisedly, up the M1. We arrived in our new house a very rag-tag bunch, sure that our new neighbours were going to think us Ridirí an Bhóthair. Indeed, after the van was parked outside the house for a week a policeman arrived at the door in response to a complaint by a neighbour, or perhaps, to be kind, it was in response to a query as to whether it had been abandoned there. I got rid of it by giving it to some local teenagers who wanted to play with it in a field.

I did not join the new branch straight away. I went to Manchester Foreign Branch on a three-month training stint which opened up nearly all the activities of a foreign branch to me. A vivid memory from that time is of returning home one Friday evening to find May in tears, having just heard the news of President Kennedy's assassination. It was fun setting up the branch from scratch with a small team of nice people. I was gaining new experiences, but the small size of the operation after the wide-open spaces in Chief Foreign and its many characters, together with an old-style manager called Potts, was less than ideal. I didn't have a memorable time there, especially after I got a page-long 'potty' letter from Potts telling me that I had better watch myself as I had overdrawn my account at the branch by five shillings (c.40 cents). The good news was that our second daughter, Margaret, was born in April 1964. She was premature and tiny and gave us some anxious moments for a while.

Harps GAA
London 1958

BACK HOME

At last, in spring 1965 I got an opportunity to get home to Ireland. I got a job as a founding member of Citibank in Dublin. The day in May that I exited Barclays Bank for the last time I walked down the pavement kicking my heels for joy at the happier prospects now before me. We shipped our few bits and pieces off, and followed by train and boat. The condition of both the trains to Holyhead and the ferries at that time were as primitive as they had been in nineteen fifty-six. On the trains you more often than not stood, or sat on your case, in a packed corridor. The ferry was a barely converted cattle boat which even the cattle would complain about if they could communicate. After a short period in Ballinvalley we rented a house in Baldoyle and a new life began.

May was heavily pregnant with Peter during all this toing-and-froing and it was a hard time for her. He was born on July ninth. I was under pressure just being part of a new team in a new situation as was natural, but we settled in quickly and faced into the future with optimism.

The culture in Citibank was entirely different from Barclays. Barclays was an 'old boy' network type of place, Citibank was a meritocracy. In Barclays, too many promotions depended on external factors that had nothing to do with merit. The outstanding guys in the provincial setup complained regularly about being passed over continually in favour of people of much less ability but with the right accent and the right connections. As we found soon enough, in Citibank if you did a good job you were moved on to the next level at the first opportunity, and on and on. Of course in a growth situation you can do that, and that is certainly what we were experiencing. By May 1966, we had had time to get everyone trained, to have thoroughly researched the market, the regulatory situation, who the movers and shakers were and what the competition had to offer, when the competition allowed themselves to be hit with a strike lasting almost 3 months. We had nearly two years growth in that period and our public profile became extraordinarily high. The bank personnel numbered about thirty-five but they did the work of seventy-five during the course of the strike. Every day was a twelve hour one and towards the end of the week we would be dragging a bit. I was not getting my usual exercise so I bought a bike and enjoyed the ten-mile trip to and from Baldoyle – it kept me in fine fettle.

Founder members of Citibank (then FNCB), Dublin, 1965: Pat O'Sullivan, Brian McConnell, Noel Ryan, Ray Leahy, Hazel Watchorn, Ross Kelly, John Lane, Maggie Martin, Peter Tuite, Aileen Buckley, Angela O'Neill, Ray Barry, Ralph Brandt, Pat Sheerin, Mary Kennedy; Bill Fitzgerald, Frances Egginton, Jim Duffy, John Cook, Jack Stanley, Don Finney, Dan Swisher, Ed Powell, Des Doyle, Mick Brophy, Phil Sheridan, Joan Barnwell

There were boxes of cash scattered all over the place and everyone except the manager spent time counting and bundling in readiness for lodgement to the Central Bank or paying out to customers for their wages. We had no vault in the building so we purchased a huge safe of about six foot square and located it in full view in the centre of the banking hall. It was not only in full view, it was floodlit. As a security measure the arrangement was effective. The safe was delivered by horse-drawn dray, much to the merriment of the New York head office personnel when they saw a photograph of the delivery in the press.

For a time we took in Irish cheques for safekeeping, and sometimes as security for emergency loans. But we ran out of space very quickly and had to refuse any more requests. These cheques, drawn on the strikebound Irish banks could not be cleared until the banks reopened. Businesses with exports were in a nice situation. They issued non-clearable Irish cheques to their suppliers and lodged their foreign ones on deposit with us. A contemporary of mine back in 1948 in St Finian's who had a small export business telephoned one day looking for banking service and by chance got me. He couldn't believe his luck and by the end of the strike he had over six hundred thousand pounds on deposit.

Another customer we gained was a Frenchman who first came into the bank with all his pockets stuffed with large franc notes. As the only French speaker in the office I dealt with him exclusively then and for several years afterwards. He was an antique dealer who had been doing so well out of his Irish purchases that he loved coming over once a year for what he described as the best comedy show he ever attended. He was an extrovert with a highly developed sense of humour and I would love to have been the fly on the wall as he dealt with his laughter-inducing Irish suppliers. He and I got on very well and we greeted each other enthusiastically when he arrived each year. The bank also enjoyed a nice profit on the foreign exchange! We experienced some startling and many merry incidents during the course of the strike, but they are better revealed over a pint and in the company of the few survivors who are still around and can still remember.

Jottings of a Country Boy

After a year renting in Baldoyle we bought a new house in Rathfarnham, funded by a soft loan from the bank. The bonus that I got after the strike came in handy for equipping the house! Around this time I was enticed back to the rugby field by one of my colleagues, Jack Stanley. He had played fly-half for Leinster in his younger days and was continuing to enjoy the odd run-out with Wanderers Rugby Club. I thoroughly enjoyed my final six years of rugby, playing for Wanderers' third team until I was thirty eight. I used to cycle over to Ballsbridge in spring and autumn with Eamon on the crossbar and Mary on the carrier to the rear. It warmed me up for the game and warmed me down afterwards. We won one championship during that time, beating our opponents in the final in a well-attended Donnybrook, the Leinster home ground at that time. A Citibank team with Pat O'Sullivan and me playing at full back and Dermot Desmond at centre back won the inaugural 'Non-associated banks' seven-a-side soccer tournament during that period. I was, of course, back playing Gaelic for Oldcastle. The same Pat O'Sullivan came down to Navan with me as a 'ringer' when Oldcastle was playing there one evening in a challenge game, and he made a great contribution to our victory.

Our third daughter, Helen was born in November 1967. We lost her once three years later during holiday time in Wexford. We were staying in Curracloe, a great spot for a family holiday that was five or six miles up the coast north of Wexford. We had driven into Wexford, done our shopping and loaded up for the return journey. May, with baby Patrick on her knee, asked in a slightly distracted way if everyone was there and we set off for home. Halfway there May said "Helen!!! Helen – where's Helen?" Sure enough she wasn't with us. A panic-stricken return to Wexford had us all walking the streets enquiring of pedestrians and shopkeepers if they had seen a little girl. We were slightly relieved to learn that she had been seen, looking into letterboxes and going into sweet shops to stare for a bit at the shopkeepers. We finally found her in a back street where she was knocking on doors. We were wobbly-kneed with relief. We also managed to lose Patrick as a two year old in Georges Street in Dublin, and Finian as a three-year-old years later when he disappeared from Clery's during a shopping trip. We were lucky that they were found within thirty minutes.

Our time in Rathfarnham was a happy one. Helen, Patrick and Anne were born during that period. We were at the foot of the Dublin Mountains and we spent many happy hours trekking up there in the heather. Anyone of the family who could walk participated. I was constantly surprised at the stamina shown by the little ones. One day when we had parked at Torc waterfall and walked up about three miles along the river which fed it, young Peter started limping. He complained of a sore ankle. He was a big heavy lump of a four year old, but I threw him up on my back and we set off back to the car. I did not need to go to the gym that day! I lowered him when we got to the car park and the little brat ran off gleefully without the slightest trace of a limp!

Rathfarnham Family

We made excursions to Ballinvalley regularly, where we let the children loose on the calves, sheep, chickens and even the gander. They played about with Neddy's successor as I had with Neddy years before. I joined them once to demonstrate how to mount the donkey from the rear, John Wayne-style. I overdid it, landed over the donkey's head and sprawled embarrassingly on the grass to gleeful howls of laughter from the little villains. Children love to see their Daddies make fools of themselves. Opposite our house in Rathfarnham there was a stream running down from the mountains in which Eamon often caught trout. The water was about six or seven feet below ground level. I saw Eamon and Mary once trying to cross the stream by means of a large branch which straddled it, so of course I proceeded to demonstrate to them the correct way to do so. Over I go on my belly as far as the centre where I came in contact with some slippery substance. Eamon reminds me that I seemed to be a long time falling with an elongated word that sounded like "Sh!!!!!!!!!!t" as I disappeared into the water below. They were rolling around with laughter above, once they were satisfied that I was ok.

In 1968 I was sent to London on a three-month credit analysis course run by a member of the staff there who was a magna cum laude Harvard graduate. The purpose of the course was to teach us how to analyse loan applications and to broaden our business outlook. This was a great opportunity for me and I grabbed it with both hands with the result that I graduated top of a class of fifteen. I then returned to Dublin to join the business development teams in a shared open-plan office. There I had plenty of opportunity to put into practice the theory learned in London. Part of my duties involved identifying and calling on new prospects. This often involved two or three consecutive days beating the bushes all over Ireland.

We always went in pairs like the Jehovah's Witnesses. Once Ron Geesy, a native of Pennsylvania Dutch territory, and I were on such a trip in Mayo. We struck up a conversation with a local banker as we waited for a table in the Breaffy House hotel. We did not reveal our business to him. He soon launched into a diatribe against the upstart American banks for trawling the countryside with hundreds of salesmen to steal clients from the Irish banks. Once he got that out of his system we had a very pleasant chat as he was a nice fellow. Ron had book matches in his pocket with the FNCB logo on it (Citibank was then known as 'The First National City Bank'), and when we were parting he could not resist handing one to him. It was cruel to subject the poor fellow to such a huge embarrassment. One of Ron's greatest delights when on the road was stopping on quiet country roads to ask people, especially children, for directions. He loved the accents and the Irish way of giving directions so much that we made a number of unscheduled stops whenever he spotted someone in the distance ahead. Once when on a trip with Roger Parsons, a very nice English lad, we called on a textile company somewhere in west Cork that our research had indicated might be worth a visit. There was no one in the office when we entered so we continued on into the factory. There was no activity and some looms were lying idle. We crept as quickly as we could towards the exit, hoping we could get away before being spotted. Just as we reached the door we were hailed from within. We introduced ourselves a little shamefacedly to be met with "F…ing bankers! How timely, come on in". We extricated ourselves from there as graciously as we could. The poor man had had a good business but obsolescence and cheap Far East imports had brought failure.

In 1970 I was sent off to America on a familiarisation and culture month-long trip. The first fortnight was spent in Head Office. While there I made sure to introduce myself to anyone that I thought I might have dealings with back in Ireland. I made some great contacts, especially major customer account officers who dealt with American companies who were already in Ireland or were planning to establish an operation there. For the second fortnight I was sent out on a road trip to Florida with nine other lads in two big cars. It was a great experience. We set out in early March through a winter-desolate New Jersey, experienced spring in Richmond, Virginia, and full summer in Jacksonville, Florida. The composition of the group was four New York staff, of whom two were Irish, and six overseas lads, one each from Paris, Geneva, Zurich, Berlin, Quito in Ecuador and Dublin.

The local lads' job was to do all the driving and keep the rest of us out of trouble while giving us a good time. Their idea of a good time was to whizz past historical sites and stop at watering holes. We let them away with that initially but as the miles flew by we, the overseas lads, decided that if we wanted to visit a place of cultural interest we were going to do so (if we were aware of one). We discovered as we visited various cities that our hotel was never in the centre, which was where we wanted to be, and finally, on our second last stop, we refused to book in to the nominated remote hotel and insisted that we should go instead to the one adjoining Cocoa Beach close to Cape Kennedy. Both hotels were Holiday Inns so there was not a problem with the change. We had an active and enjoyable time there, playing beach football, going for a boat trip up the river and stealing oranges with some trepidation from a hundred-acre orange grove.

We finished off our trip with a conducted tour of the space centre. At that time I think all of the space activity was centred there. We got close up to the self-levelling shifter that moved the upright rocket from the assembly area to the launch pad and we took a lift up to the capsule at the top of the rocket. It was dizzyingly high and of absorbing interest. I can't remember which Apollo number it was, it may have been Apollo 13. On the grounds there was an open-air museum displaying some of the capsules which had returned from space. Earlier we had spent a day in Daytona Beach. When I returned to Ireland I learned too late that three girls from around Oldcastle whom I had known well as we grew up were based in Daytona. One was a sister of Tom McDonnell and another of FX O'Reilly. They were nuns in the Sisters of Mercy order. They would have been delighted to see me as I would have been to see them. Further south we were entertained at dinner by a pianist who was hidden from view behind some flowers. When I saw him I recognised another Oldcastle person. He was Tommy Lynch of the ballroom Lynches. One of his sisters-in-law was a cousin of mine. We had a great chat and he played any type of music our group wanted to hear. He was a fine pianist.

International Citibankers in Florida 1970

On the journey down from New York to Florida we visited some of Citibank's major clients. In Boeing we got to stand upright in one of their engines, in American Tobacco I got slapped on the wrist for asking an awkward question about health in the workplace. "Bloody Irish, always asking the awkward question".

In Washington I played a game of rugby for a Georgetown university undergraduate team while my travelling companions visited museums. (A colleague in the New York office, a graduate of Georgetown University, with whom I became friendly, made the arrangements). For dinner, I was an honoured guest of a small group of Irish American post-grad students from the mid-west. Their ancestors would have arrived in America in the eighteen hundreds, possibly off famine ships. These lads were from wealthy families, were 'well' educated but while they knew everything about the mid-west they were appallingly ignorant about the rest of the world. While it was a positive sign that they took the trouble to entertain this Irishman, only one of them knew approximately where Ireland was. That is not to say that they were not good company – we had a most enjoyable evening and I am sure we learned quite a lot about each other as the wine flowed.

We had dinner in Richmond on St Patrick's Day and easily persuaded the attendant entertainers to play and sing 'Danny Boy' and a couple of other Irish tunes. The following weekend we were in Atlanta to attend the St Patrick's Day parade and enjoy the hundreds of lovely black children sitting on floats with flashing smiles. That evening we drank green beer in an Irish pub in Underground Atlanta. At the very end we spent a couple of days in Miami before flying back to New York. The most memorable sight we saw there was the many hundreds of students from cold northern universities making out on the beach.

Back in the office I took under my tutelage a young David Went who subsequently had a fine career in banking and insurance. David was very confident and ambitious and every few months he went up to the manager looking for a raise, stating that he was being head-hunted all over Dublin and he couldn't in conscience continue to work in Citibank at his current salary. I should think that within a year he was earning at least as much as I was. We enjoyed working together for a year or so. Sometime before David arrived I had to move over to the Money Desk due to the extended absence of the regular dealer. In those early days we were not properly set up with a sophisticated phone system. Every deal had to be done on the telephone. Sometimes you would be using three telephones, only two of which would be at your desk, the other on an adjoining desk, jumping from one to the other to conclude a deal involving three different outside agencies.

Banking was not a simple business where you took in money from depositors, lent it out to borrowers and you had loads of dosh hanging about just for the sake of it. The job of the 'Money Desk' as we called it was to ensure that we always had enough funds to meet our daily outflows and to invest overnight any surplus. Our largest source of funds was the money market, mostly banks lending to and borrowing from each other. In between the banks there were money brokers who were able to match one bank's need with another's surplus for a fee of, maybe, one sixteenth or one thirty-second of one percent. The daily volume was so huge that the brokers prospered on these thin margins. If a large borrower's interest rate was to be tied to the standard inter-bank rate, you would borrow from the interbank market, perhaps at a set time in the day, and book it to the customer at a margin over your borrowing rate. The Central Bank monitored the interbank rate and published it as an average of the sometimes volatile daily rates. This enabled the commercial borrower to check that his bank was applying the correct margin to his loan.

In a later life when I had turned from gamekeeper to poacher I discovered that the standard of accuracy, or even integrity, in some of the banks left something to be desired. One bank, now defunct, generally and illegally widened its profit margin, sometimes without the awareness of the lending officer. This was done by the simple expedient of the money desk, also a profit centre, adding a bit before passing it on to the lending officer. I once brought to the attention of one of their lending officers that the rate charged to their client was out of line with the interbank rate as set out in the terms of the loan and he exclaimed "The bastards", referring to his money desk colleagues   We also competed for large commercial deposits, so all in all I had to be on the ball all day every day, keeping up to date with market trends and making on-the-spot decisions. I managed the job well but it wasn't my thing and I was glad when my colleague returned.

We sometimes got prospective customers arising from the social activities of the manager of the day. Not he to turn them down! "Why don't you give Peter Tuite a call – he might be able to help you". So there you are on a Monday morning with this attractive woman at your desk, smiling sweetly at you, flashing her long lashes at you and making an impossible proposition to you. Out of the corner of my eye I would be watching for the manager to peep out of his office with a big grin on his face. All part of the learning process! I became adept at gracious refusals, and on a positive note, giving good advice.

Jottings of a Country Boy

One day I got a call from An Bord Iascaigh Mhara (The Fisheries Board) enquiring whether I would talk to a fisherman from the southwest coast about a loan proposition. It must have been during another bank strike. The Board confirmed that he was 'a good lad'. The 'lad' duly arrived with a request for a loan to buy a second-hand fishing boat in Norway to replace his older, smaller boat. I liked the cut of him and I found a way to accommodate him. He nearly dropped out of his chair when I said "OK, you can have it". He went off rubbing his hands in glee and I was delighted for him. I spent the next six months chasing him by telephone around the east, south and west coasts as he chased the herring shoals. I got to know every harbour master around the coast to Galway, from which location I got the final repayment. That relationship was interesting, fun even, as I never had doubts about eventually getting the money back and I learned a lot about another way of living and working on and around our little island.

Most of the lads were keen on golf. On an outing one hot summer's day to the beautiful Woodenbridge golf course in Wicklow, I donned my football shorts after the game, shorts which I just happened to have in the car, and jumped into the river which runs through the course. My companions, none of whom had to dam a stream to get a swim, seemed to find this amusing. The water was a bit brown, but since it was coming from the boggy Wicklow hills I'd have been surprised if it were crystal clear. In fact it was coming from the direction of the old copper mines in the hills and it was poisoned with all kinds of chemicals. That night big red bumps rose all over my skin and the itch reminded me of the bad old days of Benzyl Benzoate Emulsion! The lumps did not disappear for a fortnight.

During those development years quite a few American staff had spells in Dublin. Our first manager, Dan Swisher was a nice guy, very active, very efficient. His secretary, Frances Egginton, was from Moylough, a couple of miles from my old home in Ballinvalley. It was her brother Mick who set off walking back home from Finian's with the other two Oldcastle lads. Mick emigrated to the USA and his daughter in recent times won 'The Rose of Tralee' contest. One of the earliest staff Dan hired was young

Brian McConnell. Brian was an executive trainee in the Intercontinental Hotel, where Dan was staying. Dan liked the cut of his jib and offered him a job. He started his career working with me in the front office. From there he advanced at a rate that he had reason to be happy about. He had a very successful career, climbing to the dizzy height of CEO of not one, but two financial institutions. He had received a great boost to his career when the bank sponsored him for a full time MBA in Trinity College.

Ralph Brandt was a disenchanted Texan who was educated by the Jesuits. He floated around the office giving the impression that what he was doing was not quite what the Jesuits had in mind for him.

Another American who shall be nameless was known for his meanness. He borrowed cigarettes off everyone and when someone asked him for a cigarette he would produce from his pocket a packet with only one cigarette in it and say, "Aw look! I'm on my last one". He used to smoke all day so we surmised that he kept two packets in his pockets, one for the rebuff and the other for himself! We were all on to him and I am afraid that he got asked for a fag by people who didn't even smoke!

Adrian Evans was one of our managers early on, I think succeeding Dan Swisher. He was young, intelligent and tough in an acceptable way. He was pretty ruthless editing letters drafted for him by a subordinate. He savaged two of my drafts before I recognised that he wanted information, not literature! Almost any sentence with more than ten words was too long for him. That experience improved the quality of my English. Sadly he died young, as did Roger Parsons. Roger had gone to Greece to acquire experience in shipping. He also acquired a Greek wife whom he brought back to Dublin.

We had a dining room in the bank for entertaining clients. It was in operation for a while when I discovered to my delight that the gourmet cook, Mrs Clarke, was a daughter of my Oldcastle Mrs Reynolds and a sister of Dickie's, the poor man that I upset with Mrs Wood's bicycle. I would have known her as an older girl in my young boyhood days. I remember her, her sister and two lads who were near neighbours, walking by our house on a moonlit night one summer during the war. They were singing merrily 'Roll out the barrel...' having been at a ceilidh in Oldcastle. Here I was then, some thirty years after being satisfied with a spoon of syrup from her mother, being almost as well satisfied with her daughter's lovely food. I say 'almost' because the syrup came with a little bit of love!

This brings to mind a lunch one day attended by Ross Kelly among others. The wine was poured, Ross took a sip and declared expertly "Hum! A bit frivolous"! Our guests were suitably unimpressed that we would treat them frivolously! Ross was a beer drinker and if he hadn't seen the label on the bottle he might not have known it was wine – a very good wine it was too! Ross was a 'Hill Sixteen' type of Dubliner – one could imagine him beating his chest, Tarzan style and challenging to a fight any Meathman who looked crooked at him. He had a great sense of humour and no sense of embarrassment as he told stories against himself that few others would dare to do. Ross was running a department and a new recruit was assigned to him. This man was fairly mature and hard to manage. Ross got so frustrated with him that one day he squared up to him and invited him to sort things out like a man. The recruit looked coolly at Ross, invited him to grow up and walked away.

This little fandango was witnessed by Bill Fitzgerald, the head porter, who approached Ross to tell him that he had just escaped a near death experience. This recruit had been a Palestinian policeman at a time when they were regularly killing people in the course of their duties. To discommode Ross even more, Bill, with barely concealed relish, related a story of the recruit in action. Prior to joining Citibank the recruit had been a collector for a finance company. His job was to chase down and collect monies due and /or to recover the vehicle that had been financed. He had been trying to find a customer, a traveller, who was not honouring his contract. He bided his time as he knew where he could find him later on in the year. When the Puck Fair was on in Killorglin he headed down there, trawled the pubs and sure enough there was his man sitting drinking in the company of a man and a woman. He sauntered over and said "There you are Tommy, could I ha.......agh" – the woman had a grip of our man in a tender spot! He didn't hesitate, he gave her a vicious backhander, chopped the aggressive Tommy to the ground and sent the other fellow sprawling with a rabbit punch. He then coolly removed Tommy's wallet from his pocket, counted out the amount due plus a little for the inconvenience. He replaced the wallet and said to the onlookers "It's ok folks, I've just been collecting a debt that the man owes me. When he comes round would you please tell him that I shall be in the pub up the road if he wishes to see me".

Ross had been listening goggle-eyed to this, getting paler and paler and he had to sit down. When he had recovered somewhat he made a beeline to Hartigan's pub a short distance away. I happened to pass by Bill shortly after and he related the story briefly to me with ill-concealed humour. I found Ross slumped over two pints at the bar and I asked him what was wrong. "Jaysus, Peter, I've just had a narrow escape from being murdered" and he proceed to tell all. He genuinely felt that he had had a lucky escape.

At one time an American assistant manager spent some time with us. He was a bit of an enigma but normally he was good company. He joined a funny commune when he went back to America never to be heard from again. One of our own, Phil Sheridan went to America where she worked in the bank for a while. My information was that she too joined some sect and disappeared from the radar. We did learn that this sect sequestered her wage and in return maintained her and no doubt filled her poor head with foolishness. Phil was our telephonist and telex operator. One day she called me in a panic. She was getting messages in French from our Paris office via telex which required immediate answers as they hung on. I gave them all the answers they required and everyone was happy. Dan Swisher was also happy as the next morning he sent me a copy of the long telex with the notation "Bien fait hier avec le francais". It was nice to have recognition of an extra skill and that little bit of correspondence in my file would undoubtedly be a help when promotion was being considered.

Des Doyle, also one of our own who had worked in a New York bank before joining us in nineteen sixty-five, was thought of by the rest of us as 'the Elephant Man' because of his fabulous memory. He was a great colleague and friend and even in his late eighties his memory is impressive. When I returned from the credit analysis course in '68 the first job I got was from Des. He gave me a thick file and said "Analyse that", that being an application for additional finance for a company which had constant cash flow problems. I was doing all the analysis as learned on the course when I discovered that the company had been in Ireland for nine years and had never made a profit. I gave it the thumbs down, more on the basis of common sense than because of any sophisticated analysis. We breathed a sigh of relief when they left us and found another lender. Sure enough, within a couple of years they folded.

A great example of meritocracy at work was a young man, Noel Ryan, who escaped whatever dead-end job he had and took a job with us in the post room. This was literally and figuratively in the basement. He got the opportunity after a while to go to the book-keeping/accounts department. Soon he was in charge of that and he moved nicely in an upward trajectory. He was Personnel manager before he moved on to another bank. He retired from that bank years later as a senior director.

So, all was well, we were in the seventies, the economy was healthy, the career path was upward and my family was also expanding. Our seventh child, Anne was born in January nineteen seventy-one and later that year I was informed that I was manager designate for a new branch which would be opened in Cork in the following year. In due time we sold our house in Rathfarnham and put the profit into another new house overlooking the river in Monkstown in Cork. The house was a few minutes' walk from the school, the golf course where I took up golf, and the harbour where Eamon took up sailing.

I played rugby and Gaelic football through to spring nineteen seventy-two but I was just marking time as I had too much on my mind organising things for the Cork branch. This was to open in summer nineteen seventy-two. My last meaningful rugby was at the end of the rugby season in the previous year. I captained a team to the final of the Wanderers' seven-a-side competition. This took place in Lansdowne Road. During the course of the game one of my contact lens became detached and everyone involved in the game, including the referee, spent time on their hands and knees looking for it. We did find it and play resumed. Our opposing team had a nice blend of young flyers and old heads. Five of their team were ex internationals – the two Kavanagh brothers, the two Doyle brothers and that mighty warrior from the midlands, Gerry Culleton whom I had seen years before score a try in Twickenham from a ball bouncing off a post. They were too good for us and we lost with honour.

I continued to play Gaelic for Oldcastle up to departure for Cork. In spring seventy-two the club organised a dinner and presentation for me and gave me a good send-off. For twenty-five or -six years on and off I had donned their colours. But my GAA career did not end there. We were only a short time in Monkstown when some of the local lads set about reorganising a defunct club in the area. They did all the regulatory stuff and then organised a practice game. I willingly participated in that game on the understanding that that would be it – I was retired. After the game the management approached me and said "You're playing". I said, "I'm not". "You have to, you're captain". I went on to play for another four years and had my last competitive game at the age of forty two.

All the energy and enthusiasm that I put into these two games over the years were an enjoyable balancing activity to my dedicated work practices. I never had time to be depressed or even sorry for myself and I was privileged to share game time with some great people. I would recommend the lifestyle to any young fellow.

JNIOR A CHAMPIONS, 1966. Front row (l-r): M. McEnroe, H. McCluskey, B. Gilsenan, J. McEnroe, Sheridan, B. Heatherton, M. Devine, B. Hamill (RIP), A. Galligan, J. Tynan, Fr. B. Halpin, K. Tynar, Mahon. Back row: J. Sheridan, P. Smith (RIP), J. Gilsenan (RIP), N. Mahon, P. Culligan, P. Pursel, P. Tuite, B. Smith, J. Rahaill, O. Lynch, P. Kearney, J. Smith, J. Rahaill (Sen).

Oldcastle Junior A Champions 1966

Wanderers Rugby Club third team c.1971

Non-associated Banks 7-a-side Soccer Champions 1971
Pat Sullivan, Peter Tuite, Carl Manzi, Rodney Allsop, Tommy Stormer;
Jim Galvin, Bobo Boland, Mick O'Mahoney, Donie Kerrin, Dermot Desmond

CORK

Apart from my secretary, Helen Nolan, who was local, I sourced all my staff from Dublin branch, now my local Head Office. We were a wholesale office with relatively low volumes so we did not need too many people. Jim Farrell was my assistant manager. He was competent and committed and we got on well together. Dermot Desmond was my complete credit department. This was a key department where loans and other risk assets were researched and processed. Dermot was a likeable young lad who always had the ears cocked and was ready to advance his knowledge by drawing on other people's experience. He did a good job and I was sorry to lose him when he moved back to Dublin. None of us at that time had any inkling that he would become a billionaire. Pat O'Sullivan, aided by Aileen Buckley who was originally from Passage West, was in charge of Operations. This involved the internal workings of the office in terms of processing transactions and dealing with accounting and bookkeeping matters as well as looking after the day-to-day needs of our clients. Pat and I had played both Gaelic and soccer together in the past. Henry the porter also chanced leaving Dublin for Cork.

With Avery Chope and Headoffice executives at the opening of FNCB branch, Cork, 1972

Aileen's father, Michael, had a pub in Passage West, just down the road from Monkstown. One night when we were expecting two of my colleagues for dinner I popped down there for some mixers. Michael insisted on introducing me to a wee man sitting in the corner. He had a glass of what I thought would be rum in front of him. (It turned out to be an innocuous sherry). "This is Martin Corry, he is with us this evening to draw the raffle ticket" – it was the culmination of a big charity event. "What are you drinking"? "Aw Martin, I'd love to have a drink with you but I have to go back to my guests". "Sit down Boy". I sat down. Eight whiskeys later my guests arrived to rescue me! (Spare a thought for poor May left to deal with eight children, to cook, and to entertain my guests). The first whiskey was a show of bravado to match Martin's 'hard likker', the rest just flowed from that. That I managed eight whiskeys without falling off the chair was a tribute to my constitution since, with the exception of a very occasional gin & tonic and some wine at meals, I did not drink at all. I had known of Martin by reputation – that's why I sat down, although at the back of my mind I had the thought that I could learn some inside information about the activities of the Irish guerrillas who annoyed the British around Cork during the War of Independence. Martin had been a senior figure in the East Cork brigade of the IRA. He had a fearsome reputation for daring deeds and occasional ruthlessness. So the stories began.

It appeared that Martin was very daring and he loved doing the unexpected when confronted with the British soldiers. If they had intelligence that he might be in a particular place, Martin would be there, but out in the open as a delivery man or some other obviously innocent person. On one occasion the British had intelligence that Corry was going to be at Kent railway station to coincide with the arrival of the Dublin train. The British put all their available resources to surveillance of the station and surroundings. Tension was building. Suddenly a horse and trap pulled up to the platform entrance and a little becapped man hopped down, whistling. He lifted a milk churn off the trap, carried it over to the platform, left it there, returned to his trap and trotted away. The British surveillance was still looking out for Martin long after he had trotted down the road and out of sight.

Jottings of a Country Boy

When the IRA were on an operation and wanted to get past an army blockade they would sometimes lie on top of a scheduled bus and make their way undetected. The old buses then had crating on their tops for luggage which offered good concealment.

Martin's ruthlessness was shown in the next story. The east Cork brigade was going through a period of intense activity, matched by equally intense activity by the British. Some Tommies went wild, dragged three teenage boys from three homes known to be associated with the IRA and bayoneted them before throwing them over a cliff. Martin gave instructions: All future activities were to be devoted exclusively to the capture of the commander of the British forces in the area. Eventually they did get him and Martin chaired a court martial. (Not a trial, he was keen to emphasise). Martin addressed the officer. "Now Commander, we are both soldiers and we try to stick to certain well-recognised standards when it comes to women and children – we do not make war on them. You are being court-martialled now, not because you are an opposing soldier, you are being tried for being responsible for an atrocity against innocent children. What do you have to say?" The officer knew that even if he had the eloquence of Churchill it would not save him so he went out with flags flying. "F... you". "I slammed my fist on the table, said 'Guilty', marched him out, put him against a wall and shot him myself".

A boast Martin made had to do with politics in the thirties. Apparently there was a two-day debate in the late thirties in the Dáil on the matter of settling the dispute with Britain which had caused the Economic War. During the debate the Northern Irish situation was raised. Martin said that after listening to nonsense for hours on end "I got up and said: 'I was in Crumlin Road [the jail in Belfast] in nineteen twenty-something – there were only two Northerners there. They're no good, any of them. The only solution is to mobilise poison-gas canisters at the border, wait for a following wind and gas the whole lot of them and then start all over again'. There was uproar, but you know at the next election I got in with an increased majority of nine thousand"!

What an interesting way to purchase a few mixers! Actually I never got to do that. My colleagues got me safely back to the house, which I managed to enter in an upright position. I never did get a chance to check out Martin's stories other than the poison gas bit – there was no Google then!

We all worked hard at making the branch 'grow' as modern phraseology expresses it. I was working hard and as smart as possible to keep abreast of new inward investment. Ireland had come out of a deep sleep as a result of Whittaker and Lemass-inspired action in the sixties. Dublin and Cork were alive with businessmen from America and Europe investigating the suitability of Ireland as a location for production facilities, or having already done that, trying to identify a good location to site a factory. I had one of the receptionists at the principal hotel in Cork primed to call me when American and German corporate guests booked in. On learning the names I would immediately telex one of the guys in HO or Stuttgart that I had met on my visits there. He, or the appropriate account officer, would contact the prospect's headquarters to remind them that we had a presence in the area and we were anxious to offer support. Our HO account officers loved getting such telexes from me as it invariably helped them to cement relationships with an existing client and to create new business from non-customers. Sometimes American corporations who had sent envoys secretly to Ireland were astonished that Citibank were well aware of their presence there.

The international aspect of our banking business was heavily emphasised. If a customer had a problem in another country or countries we had a presence there to help them sort it out. I once had a perfect example of this. One of our international customers had a cross-border difficulty relating to the activities of its Italian, Swiss and Irish operation. With the approval of the Irish company I arranged a meeting on the Continent with the Irish finance director, his counterpart in his head office, this man's boss and three Citibankers – officers from the Milan and Zurich branches and myself. It was a complex situation and we spent the best part of a day working on it with very satisfactory results. The problems were solved and the company head man had complimentary things to say about us and about how important it had become for them to have an international bank of our standing in support.

On the business development front I was very active locally, calling regularly on customers and prospects. I did not succeed in getting business from everyone but I still made it a point to visit some of my more interesting prospects once a year in order to develop friendly relations with the management. We would know, as would the management, that as things stood there was little prospect of business in the short term but all kinds of events could change that. There was one prospect in Cork that I had been calling on annually for nine years, in that time developing a friendship and no business. One day when walking down Grafton Street I bumped into their two senior managers and before we parted I had agreed to provide them with a service, profitable to us, which their own bank could not handle. Persistence pays if there is a bit of luck thrown in! A notable one that got away from us and is now a multibillion agri/food business was a start-up, undercapitalised and trying to build the business on borrowings. Jim Farrell and I liked the pair who were launching the business but we had to turn them down on the basis that they were under-capitalised.

In nineteen seventy-four I did an energy-sapping trip to America, calling on the HO of existing customers and on others I had identified as prospects. I reckoned that I did twenty thousand miles all over the country. After liaising with the account officers in my HO I set out on my travels to see more financial directors in two weeks than I would see in the six months thereafter. I got a warm reception from all existing clients and I was pleasantly surprised at how useful I was to some very high ranking directors who had not a clue about some aspects of the regulatory and financial environment that their Irish operations were working in. With prospects the reception was always friendly and there was strong interest in hearing about conditions in Ireland from an Irishman. From a business viewpoint the trip was a success, despite the fact that I drew some blanks. One of those was a trip I made to San Diego, miles south of Los Angeles to visit there a tuna processing company that had been reported to be setting up an operation in Drogheda. When I got there they knew nothing about it and it never did happen. I drove for the first time in America on four and five lane highways out of Los Angeles. That was terrifying and I was lucky to survive.

On my first morning in Los Angeles I arrived down to the hotel lobby at an early hour and the first person I saw there was Jack Stanley, my rugby playing ex-colleague from Citibank Dublin. He was also hustling, but now for an Irish bank. In Chicago on my way to the airport my taxi had a blowout that had the driver struggling to remain on the road and I had to wave down a passing car to take me to the airport. The driver, a nice young fellow dropped me at the departure door and made nothing of it. Heart-warming!

In Detroit I had arrangements to meet one of my American cousins and her mother in the airport on the way through, but my inward flight was delayed and we could only have a breathless conversation on the way to the next flight. I suppose I was a bit in panic mode and the thinking, if there was any at all, was inadequate for the occasion. Of course I should have rescheduled, spent the night with them and headed off the next day, or maybe even the following one. I had never met my Uncle Bill's widow who was from Sligo, and I was not to meet my cousin Elizabeth again for many years. It was galling that the business meeting I was rushing to turned out to be a waste of time.

While in San Francisco I visited my brother Michael who was living in Palo Alto at the time. I played golf with a mover and shaker, also in Palo Alto, who had two Rolls in the garage and a 'fled' wife. In Jacksonville a customer arranged a game of golf for me at Ponte Vedra Golf and Country Club. Ponte Vedra beach is very close to the famous Sawgrass course belonging to the PGA. In Tallahassee I was a guest of a client. A fellow guest was an Important legal person and his wife. Some of the conversation touched on the treatment of 'blacks' and I sure wouldn't want to be a black person in Florida! I was telling the wife about how much I had enjoyed the St Patrick's Day Parade in Atlanta on my previous trip in 1970, especially the hundreds of lovely black children with their happy laughter. She said, and I quote "How could you think black children were lovely?" In deference to my host I kept my temper in check and let it pass (coward?).

Before retiring for the night I mentioned to my host that I needed to get to mass the following morning. He made a phone call and soon a middle-aged man with an Irish name entered. "McNulty, you go to Mass every Sunday, don't you? Good. Will you take Mr Tuite to Mass in the morning, you know the time I'm sure". My host knew that McNulty hardly ever went to Mass and that he had no idea what time it was at. "Yes sir, Mr___, no problem." The next morning we headed off and my new-found driver seemed very hesitant, slowing down as he passed by each church. Finally he drew into the parking lot of a fine white-painted church, locked the car and we were almost at the steps when a smiling clergyman emerged. McNulty swore: "It's *=# Baptist" and turned abruptly back to the car with a bemused me lagging behind. We finally found the church – a red brick building. It was full to overflowing, but not one black person was to be seen. I suppose it is easy to see that as a complete failure of the Catholic Church in the area to fulfil its Christian mission. At the same time I was beginning to understand how difficult it must have been then for a decent white person to go against the herd and behave properly towards black people.

While in Tallahassee I met the sheriff of Dade County, a place that had gained notoriety in the past for reasons I now forget although I think it had to do with multiple murders. He had a murderous looking forty-five revolver in his holster and a red neck. Very bravely I asked him what he thought of black people. "Well. It's like this: when my dogs are about me if I'm in good humour I pat them, if I'm in bad humour I kick them, does that answer your question?" At the end of my trip I spent a couple of days with my sister Cella and her family in Long Island.

With my niece Karen and nephew Sean in Long Island 1974

FRUIT FARMING

While in Cork I got involved in a small speculative investment with a friend, his brother and my brother Pat. With strong prospects for the expansion of Ringaskiddy industrial area we purchased fifteen acres of land close by as a medium- to long-term speculation. We decided that we should produce something on the land in the meantime. Under advice from a horticulturalist we decided that it was a perfect location climate-wise for soft fruit production. Roche's Point, just across the harbour, had a climate very close to that in Southampton, one of the sunniest places in the UK. We prepared the soil under direction of John Joe Costin the horticulturalist, and planted twelve acres of strawberries and two of raspberries. We hired a special piece of equipment on which two children sat and as it was pulled along the drills the children planted the plants on the aperture created by the machine. In the spring I hammered in eight-foot long stakes twelve feet apart on the drills for tying up the growing raspberry plants. The second year we had a full crop and then we got into something we had not given much thought to – the picking and distribution of the fruit.

Think of collecting and managing one hundred children and delivering them home again on time, and you will have no idea of the difficulties involved. Think of dropping your own children on a half dozen roads around Cork with their signs and fruit, and collecting them in the evening. Think of heading off to the Dublin fruit market at four o'clock in the morning with fifteen hundred pounds worth of early strawberries and getting back in the office for a full day's work. Think about driving that evening at ten or eleven o'clock to Newmarket in North Cork with a load for the wholesaler Cor Flynn, with young Margaret or Mary along to keep you awake by thumping you on the back or slapping you on the face. Think of handling irate parents when we would be late delivering the children back to them in the evenings. Think of suffering insults in the Southern Star newspaper from West Cork regarding exploitation of children – we were in a snake pit. Poor May had to desert her kitchen to spend exhausting hours picking up the pieces. The following year when she was heavily pregnant with Brendan she was backing out of our driveway on her way to the field without realising that her car door was open and it got ripped off on the pier. When she got to the field she made sure to enter and park in such a way that I could not see the damage! Customers and friends who were driving out to Crosshaven in the evenings for the sailing told nice stories of young nine year old Peter acting the gom and leaving it to them to pay what they thought was fair as he wasn't up to doing the calculations himself! He always got more than the set price plus many generous tips! Kevin Cotter, a neighbour, used to visit us in the evenings to help us out and on leaving he always exaggerated checking the soles of his shoes for twenty pound notes! (There would be a lot of money scattered about waiting for counting). My brother Willie and cousin Sheila spent two or three seasons working with us.

The whole business was fun at times but it was just too much on top of everything else and we eventually sold the land on after getting planning permission for housing. Years later when I had returned to Dublin, some old customers told me that I had left Cork with a bigger reputation as a horticulturalist than a banker!

Despite the sideline everything was going well with the real work, the branch was in profit and moving nicely upward. My family and I had settled in happily in Monkstown, Eamon the keen sailor, crewed for Ireland in the 505 Class in the European championships. I played football for Monkstown and spent some happy hours in and around the golf course when I was not sweating away in the garden. Batt Murphy was the professional and he became a good friend. He tried with only partial success to give me a swing, despite which I got my handicap down to six for a while. Our two youngest children, Finian and Brendan, were born in Cork and finally our family was complete. We had bought a sixteen foot ship's lifeboat soon after arriving in Cork and we spent hours motoring around the harbour.

MOVING ON

In late nineteen seventy-four I had a problem with my Dublin boss, a recently-arrived fellow called Lilycotch (If I hadn't just deleted an 'r' his name would have appeared as 'Lilycrotch). He had offered me a salary increase that I asked him to reconsider. I learned later that his thinking was that I was well settled in Cork with a big family and other opportunities would be hard to come by, so he looked after the fellows that he would be bumping into every day in his own office. At the same time Guinness and Mahon were planning to open a branch in Cork and they were in the market for a founding manager. I wasn't that interested but I put in an application anyway out of curiosity. When Lilycotch did not revert to me despite being made aware that I was considering an alternative offer, I accepted G&M's offer and telexed my resignation to Lilycotch. I also spoke to my colleagues in New York and they didn't like it at all that they were going to lose a good overseas ally for a few hundred pounds. Their boss must have got on to our big boss in London, Dick Vokey. (Dick had appointed me to the position in the first place) and he got on to Lilycotch to tell him to give me whatever I wanted. (That was an increase of a mere three hundred pounds, but I never got as far as talking figures to Lilycotch, I just said that I wanted him to reconsider). Of course I could not honourably now renege on my agreement with G&M despite pressure to do so. My starting salary with G&M was four thousand pounds more than my Citibank remuneration but I would have carried on happily there for three thousand seven hundred less. I was informed later by a friend in the Dublin office that Lilycotch accused me of stabbing him in the back. Anyway, he was moved on shortly after that, and deservedly so. Of course on reflection I realised that I had not handled the matter well. I should have telephoned my contacts in New York before I accepted G&M's offer.

I got G&M's Cork branch on the road, literally, since I was as likely to be down in the depths of Kerry chasing deposits as sitting in the new South Mall office. G&M were uniquely the only 'Non-Associated', (meaning non-highstreet clearing bank), with Trustee Status. Under the legislation this meant that trustee funds, such as for example, solicitors' client accounts, could be placed on deposit with us. The high street banks had very cosy relationships with their solicitor clients, often resulting in the client account deposit being the dynamic for sweetheart deals for the solicitor personally. The problem I had was that the solicitors, while interested in our higher rates, did not want anything to interfere with the cosy arrangement. Being seen to have dealings with a competitor bank would threaten that. So the response I got from many of the solicitors was to the effect that if I could show them a way to transfer money out of their bank without the bank learning about it they would gladly enter a relationship with us. The banks in country areas knew everything that went on locally. If for instance a client of the solicitor had a property for sale, the bank would be watching to see the proceeds at least passing through them, if not deposited in a client account. In Cork itself the solicitors were not so dependent on one bank and the fact that the bigger firms would have at least two banks anyway meant that we could do business with them.

I was now in a different world from that experienced in the Citibank environment for the previous nine years. G&M was a small bank, with its London office the major player. London gave the Dublin office a fair amount of independence. Their lending business was limited in size both individually and collectively because of the low capital base of the Group. This meant for me that I had to develop a complete banking business with different size and type of client. Citibank's interest was primarily to service the needs of the multinationals flooding into Ireland at the time with the occasional large Irish corporation thrown in. We worked on the principle that every relationship should yield a certain minimum return regardless of whether it was on what we called 'money rental', a combination of money rental and ancillary business, or other non-lending profit generation activities such as foreign exchange dealing, issuing letters of credit and dealing on a fee paying basis with all kinds of documents related to paying for imports or collecting for exports. With G&M that source of business was largely closed off to us and we were forced by our size to focus on small to medium sized indigenous businesses. In the early Citibank days of calling on indigenous businesses I sometimes was close to having to put my foot in the door. The Guinness name was magic and it was invariably a "come on in" reaction. G&M was founded in 1836, two years before the first steamship left Cobh for the first crossing of the Atlantic. I had a lovely advertisement prepared to reflect on that fact. It attracted much positive comment.

One day a woman from West Cork called in to see me without an appointment. She said that she was taking the initiative to do that as her husband was a man of low ambition but lots of opportunities. He was a farmer working hard at building up a decent-sized herd of milch cows by rearing them from the suckling stage. I told her that it was not the type of business that we did so she went away. The following day she telephoned me and pleaded with me to come down and talk to her husband. I relented, and off I went to get a warm welcome from her and a considerably less enthusiastic one from him. He looked at me from under his bushy eyebrows and his peaked cap with a speculative rather than an unfriendly look. I invited him to show me the fifteen yearling heifers which he wanted financed to the calving and milking stage. I sat on the railing of a pen while he drove the young cattle in for my inspection. I complimented him on them and said that they would make great cows, but unfortunately I really could not get involved. This was the answer he wanted and as I was leaving him he could not contain his great good humour. I also had difficulty in suppressing my laughter as we parted and I could picture him in the pub that night telling his pals about the stroke he had pulled on this townie banker. I could not have spoiled his fun by letting him know that I was brought up on a farm and that in Oldcastle heifers had different appendages from those displayed by his beasts. Of the fifteen 'heifers', thirteen were bullocks!

I was busy and successful in a slow build-up of business and that kept me reasonably happy in the new environment. I had a local director, Clayton Love, who was supportive and I was getting on well with my bosses in the Dublin office, especially Michael Pender. However, I was aware of business being run out of the Dublin office related to offshore deposits and a Cayman Island operation which was questionable both from a regulatory and prudential point of view. This aspect of the business was conducted very secretively, with only two staff apart from the directors being involved. The true extent of it was only revealed much later after the media focused on the Charlie Haughey/Des Traynor relationship. In any event I was a bit nervous about it and this had an influence on me when I was headhunted by a Dublin-based bank which was recruiting a managing director. I said no initially as I thought it would be a bit unfair to desert the ship so soon, but eventually after some persistent courting by this bank's Cork-based Chairman John Ronan, I agreed to meet the directors.

BACK TO DUBLIN
The bank was Trinity Bank, a fairly new bank based on the corner of Dame Street and Trinity Street. It barely qualified for the term 'bank' at this stage, being little more than a brokerage house run by accountants and

deal makers. It was a subsidiary of Brown Shipley in London and Philadelphia National Bank which had a minority stake. Brown Shipley had been an offshoot of Brown Brothers, a trading house-cum-bank founded in the USA in the eighteenth/nineteenth century by disaffected Presbyterians from Northern Ireland. The Chairman of Brown Shipley was Lord Farnham from Cavan, just down the road from Oldcastle. It turned out that the job offer was not the Managing Directorship that John Ronan had discussed, but a 'pending' CEO position while they worked on a way to get rid of the incumbent, a man they were very unhappy with. After exhaustive discussion about how I would bring the bank into the mainstream with solid support from the shareholders, I agreed to accept the position of Banking Director pro tem with a contractual obligation on them to appoint me to the Managing Directorship within six months. It transpired that it took only a couple of months for the incumbent to disqualify himself from the job by arrogant and disruptive behaviour. I had heard whispers that he was disparaging me at every opportunity with the staff. This I pretended to be unaware of, but when he sat at my desk one day to say "Peter, you are only a little bank clerk, this job is too much for you", I said "Well let's see then". I picked up the phone, called Lord Farnham, explained what was going on and said "Barry, either this fellow goes or I do". My man's smirk disappeared and he removed himself from my office for the last time. After I got rid of another arrogant accountant there who was achieving nothing (he seemed to think that anyone who was not an accountant was an inferior being), the bank settled in to be a bank. I had Paul Cran, another (non-arrogant) accountant, and John McGilligan appointed fellow directors. John was a son of Paddy McGilligan, an ex-Fine Gael minister who was in the Dáil the day Martin Corry offered his infamous solution to all the troubles in Northern Ireland.

There was a new purpose about everyone in the office and we became an effective team. We did well despite all the restrictions imposed on us by the limited capital base of ourselves and our shareholders. We were allowed to lend a limited amount on our own books so we had to lay off any exposure over our threshold to our shareholders. This impinged on their own limits and as they regarded the transaction as pure money rental (since we got any ancillary business) they were dragging their feet a bit on it. We were obliged then to focus on smaller businesses. This inevitably led to property financing. Despite the fact that we were attempting to get involved in property lending only if there was a related commercial element to it with positive cash flow, we were aware that if a severe downturn hit the economy in a high-interest market we would encounter difficulties. I regretted later that we had not replaced the arrogant accountant with a team-playing dealmaker. I had been soured by the attitude of those fellows, and we were too strongly focused on getting a bank up and running. We were coming across the odd opportunity to put bigger deals together jointly with one or two of the local banks and there was some mergers and acquisitions business that we had to pass up for lack of expertise.

We motored along, doing well in a growth situation. The development of our bank-to-bank business necessitated visits occasionally to our European correspondent banks. These were the banks we would use to make transfers of funds abroad or to complete a variety of foreign transactions which required the cooperation of a bank in the country concerned. I had been to Denmark and Frankfurt on one such trip and in conjunction with this I had planned to return via London and to go on directly from there to New York. I had asked my secretary, Jean Tyson, to book me on the quickest flight she could from London. She booked me on Concorde! This is not what I had in mind but it turned out to be very beneficial as I was able to plan seven or eight appointments in New York for the day of my arrival there. I was met from the Frankfurt plane by a glamorous hostess who escorted me to the Concorde departure gate and on from there to the plane. On the unadjusted clock I arrived in New York before I left London and I got through my eight appointments satisfactorily. It was a demanding schedule but worth it. Concorde used to fly 60,000 feet up and from there I could see the curvature of the earth. Because of a noise problem the plane normally delayed giving the engines full boost until it was clear of all habitation and then one was pushed back in one's seat with the acceleration.

I was appointed a director of Brown Shipley. This pleased me as an affirmation that I was doing a good job and also that the directors considered that I would have a useful input into their own business. When on a trip to Zurich once with the managing director we were invited to lunch at the UBS HO (Union de Banques Suisses). To my surprise the CEO and his deputy made a fuss of me because I was a rare bird in their offices – a countryman of James Joyce. It was an eye-opener for me to witness the regard they had for Joyce, even to the extent of having a memorial to him in their building. My managing director was suitably impressed as well.

I attended monthly board meetings at Brown Shipley. The meeting was followed by lunch in their panelled dining room and I remember thinking once "Ah Dad, if you could only see me now, your little garsún from Ballinvalley, feeding at the trough with the powerful financiers of the City of London".

Over the previous few years I had made a study of the forestry business and in an attempt to get involved directly, I and some friends bought about 900 acres of suitable land outside Oughterard. We planted one hundred acres as an indication of serious intent and applied to the department for the grants that were nominally available. The forestry people did not want any private involvement in the business and despite favourable noises from the then minister, Brian Lenihan, we could make no progress, so we sold the land on at a price which just covered our outlay. It was a disappointing attitude adopted by the people involved in forestry at the time and it took quite a few years for their dog-in-the-manger attitude to be overruled.

Sometime in 1979 I got a telephone call one Friday evening on my home telephone. The caller was a reporter from the Irish Independent who wanted my comment on "The events at Trinity Bank this evening". I kicked to touch and told him that I would call him back. I then called the bank where the Special Branch were in attendance and got confirmation that there had been a robbery there. Trinity dealt in small amounts of cash only and we had rented out the vault to the security company Group 4. It appeared that around £500,000 had been stolen. The Special Branch was there because the suspects were IRA. Group 4 were minding our few punts and the security of the cash on the premises was the responsibility of that company. The Special Branch must have had an inside track because within a few hours and after a few chases around inner Dublin they had recovered most of the missing cash. We learned later that the robbers had somehow gained entry to the yard at the rear of the bank, subdued the one Group 4 staff member there, laid him on the ground and then lifted the bank's Mini car that was parked there on top of him. He was pinioned painfully there for a considerable length of time but he did not suffer serious injury. He was an Englishman, so he must have felt relieved to suffer only the treatment meted out to him as the robbers had threatened him with the name of their organisation. The day after the robbery my son Eamon met my Uncle Pee who asked him how I was getting over the robbery. Eamon said "He's probably playing golf". "Well the Canister!" said Pee.

A couple of years later Paddy, the porter in the bank, discovered a partially completed tunnel under the bank with sticks of dynamite in a dangerous condition stored there!

In the early eighties I began to take my eye off the ball. I got involved as an investor in the development of a new product. There were four of us, the inventor, who had a carried interest, and two others with myself. We, the three investors, agreed that our involvement would be on the basis that our exposure would be limited to £20,000 each. The product worked, but an amateur marketing decision was made which ensured that it would sell only in very small volumes. On foot of some bad decisions by others and no-less doubtful ones by myself the project cost me not €20,000 but £120,000, without any involvement in the management of the business.

During this time I hired Denis O'Brien as my PA to do some project work. As a graduate of Boston College he had acquired all the methodology to tackle any problem from scratch. He did some good work before departing to take up a similar position with Tony Ryan. I would have been surprised if he had not been a success, but as in the case of Dermot Desmond, I would never have expected that he would become a billionaire.

I must have reached what is called the 'Peter Principle' around this time too because I began to become unusually error prone. (The Peter Principle: "In a hierarchy every employee tends to rise to their level of incompetence").The stress began to become almost physical. To combat that I used to spend many lunch hours half killing myself in the gym. The result was that as the economy began to falter and then plunge downward in the early eighties I stopped enjoying the job. It was time for a change!

The trigger for a career change came in late December 1982 when I approved an emergency addition to a loan to two fellows from Cork. The bank had had satisfactory dealings with them for some years. The increase was somewhat above my authorised limit. I could justify the loan on a commercial basis but I was out of order. When my bosses began to make a larger fuss about it than I thought it merited I decided that the right thing to do was to resign. My offer to resign was accepted, not with alacrity I am glad to say, and I was again a free agent. While I did not kick my heels with joy exiting Trinity Bank for the last time, I did have a great sense of relief, mingled with regret that I had not done as well as I would have liked for the people who relied on me.

SELF-EMPLOYMENT AND RETIREMENT

In the period leading up to my resignation I had been doing some research on the options available to me outside of employment in an institution. I felt reasonably confident that I could make a living in financial services, in particular as a broker of loans and mortgages, on a self-employed basis. But by the time that I got involved in this the banks were not now looking for new loans – they were putting all their attention into getting money back. The downturn had already been making some headway and the prognosis was very gloomy. I put our house on the market to repay my borrowings. There were no takers and after a year or so we moved into a rented cottage down the road. This action was to show good faith to our lenders, who otherwise might be thinking that we were deliberately obstructing the sale. The house didn't sell for nearly three years, and then at half its nineteen eighty-three valuation. This meant that it covered only half my borrowings. I fortunately managed to retain a couple of acres, as the buyer was not prepared to pay the extra for the whole site. Inability to meet my obligations was probably the most painful aspect of all my troubles around that time.

I have not yet mentioned my family and the upset caused to May and the children. May of course was supportive and bore the severe disappointment and disruption with great patience. We all had to get on with it and face the changed situation bravely. Just before I resigned I, and three other members of my family opened a supermarket in Dunshaughlin. This was to be managed by one of the shareholders, my brother Pat, but two weeks before the opening he got seriously ill. We appointed an outside manager, who we had to let go after six months when we were forty thousand down. Poor May stood into the breach and the shop was operated at breakeven until we managed to sell it on to two young Fergal Quinn lads who knew the business inside out. They sold it on a couple of years later to a man who had other Supervalu brand shops.

Some years ago he got about thirty million for five shops and we speculated that his Dunshaughlin shop would have realised six million.

One of the first calls I got after I left Trinity Bank was from Dermot Desmond. He said "Now Peter, what can **I** do for **you**"? And he did put a bit of business my way. Dermot isn't just a money machine – he has a big heart as well!

The slow build-up of business in financial services and the gloomy prospects for most of the eighties forced me to rethink and in nineteen eighty-six I took to Ryanair and headed for London. I had decided that I would spend two out of every three weeks in London and the other week in Dublin. In London I got a desk and a phone and after a breaking-in period I began to do some reasonably good business. My first task there was to research the providers of finance in all its guises. The variety of products available was very welcome after the dead hand of Dublin's impoverished offerings. London was stimulating and full of potential because of the range of quirky deals that could be done for clients there that would not be possible in any other finance centre in the world.

One of my prospects was a 9 carat gold jewellery maker. He had cash flow problems as he had to buy gold upfront in minimum amounts, much more than he really needed. This was then stored in his safe with attendant security problems and expense. Through various contacts I had developed I was able to solve all his problems. First of all I got the gold supplier, under a guarantee from an insurance company, to store gold in my client's safe and to charge only for what he removed from it for his work in progress. The removal was tightly controlled. Part of the package was that I brought a bank aboard to discount his invoiced sales so that funds were available to pay for the gold removed. (Discounting invoices involves a kind of bridging finance against monies due on invoiced sales). I also put in place a requirement of the lender that the owner had to take out a term life policy for one million pounds. He was elderly and that was costly – ten thousand pounds annually. I got a nice fee for that deal which was sweetened by commission for the insurance. That package worked well for two or three years until he built up enough profits and cash flow to enable him to raise working capital in the normal way. I lost touch with him then and the next thing I got a telephone call from his accountant to tell me that my client had just died, six months after cancelling the insurance policy. I was reminded of this deal and the insurance company guarantee element of it when AIG had to be bailed out to the tune of one hundred and eighty five billion dollars in the crash, much of it to do with reckless guarantees of careless investment.

By nineteen eighty-eight, I had done well with this and some other profitable deals, mostly to do with arranging finance for individuals who may have been good at making things or selling, but with poor understanding of finance and bankers. I was able then to start thinking of building a house on the remaining acreage of the site in Dunshaughlin and building commenced in October of that year. One of the deals I had arranged was a contract for one of my old banking clients with one of the major building contractors in London. I had learned that the contractor was about to invite tenders for the cladding with granite of a major construction in the Docklands. I learned of this from the boyfriend of a good friend of mine, Terry Devine with whom I had shared an office when I first went to London in '86. Terry, from Belfast, was one of those exceptional young women who left everyone smiling behind her. Her boyfriend, Lenny Fisher, was PA to the managing director of the contracting company. He had mentioned the company's plans casually to me at a social engagement. I asked him to stall the tendering process for a few days while I contacted a cladding company that I suggested would be perfect for this contract. This company had just completed a major contract in Hastings & Hudson in New York which was of the same scale as the proposed building in Docklands.

I called the owner, Jack Fogarty of the cladding company, FEI Ltd, and asked him if he would be interested in the contract and if so, would he pay me a fee of one hundred thousand dollars for an inside track leading to swinging the deal? "Ok" he said, "I'm on the plane tomorrow". Jack and I went back to nineteen seventy-six when he was wheeled into my office in Trinity Bank by a New York lawyer contact. Jack was setting up an Irish company in Athy for the assembly of granite cladding panels for installation in high rise buildings. He was at that time preparing to get production up and running for the assembly and fixing of granite clad walls to an Olympia & York high rise commercial building in New York. He had negotiated all the assistance that he could from Irish state agencies but he was short a fairly modest amount of funding. The deal looked ok and I told him he could have the money subject to this, that and the other. He was impressed and delighted, and Trinity got a good client for a few years. I am sure the lawyer got a nice fat commission from Jack for a half hour's networking.

Lenny and Terry were not expecting a fee from FEI as that would create a conflict of interest. However, I had been promised a fee and I told them I would share it with them fifty/fifty. All that was required from Lenny was a well-researched presentation to his managing director and a gentle hand on the tiller now and again. Jack got the contract but he didn't pay the fee. Instead he hired Lenny and me at one hundred thousand dollars each per year, I as managing Director of his Irish company and Lenny as a roving trouble-shooter.

So, after a visit to FEI's New York headquarters, Jack flew back with me First Class, the first and only time that I had that experience, and I was installed as the third or fourth MD since the operation started. I was well aware that Jack was difficult to work for through my experience dealing with a succession of MDs in my Trinity days. All of these quit suddenly, sometimes acrimoniously, with Jack blaming them for all his troubles. A few months later he would be regretting their loss! I was also well aware that smallish family companies can be a difficult place to work at a management level, so it was no surprise to me when this proved to be so in my case. However, I reckoned that if I lasted six months I would get enough money together to build my house so I soldiered on. The business was difficult, mainly because we were in a cyclical industry, and if a new contract was not in place to dovetail with the completion of the previous one we could have two hundred workers standing around idle, earning money that the company was not. The situation called for a very flexible employment policy that ensured that there was a fair allocation of the available work. Jack was a blunt instrument and management-worker relations were generally hostile, an uncomfortable position for me. I was the opposite of Jack, who was confrontational. He would interfere from New York, countermanding some of my instructions, occasionally without informing me. His modus operandi was to solve one of today's problems by creating two for tomorrow. I called it "the shoot yourself in the foot management style". Somebody other than Jack, however, had more often than not to bear the pain. The building in the London Docklands that FEI clad was afterwards blown up by the IRA.

There was a lot of surplus sheets of polished granite lying about in the factory yard. Jack gave me the ok to remove some of it to my new house. The flooring and worktops are still in place twenty-five years later. The granite was not free however, as when I parted company with some minor acrimony, Jack stopped my final salary payment, declaring when I raised objection: "Well, you got the granite"! During my time there, a total of a little over seven months, I was headhunted by a recruitment agency for one of the major financial institutions in Dublin to head up a new project. I had resolved when I left Trinity Bank that I should avoid working for an institution again if at all possible, so I declined. My attitude to being involved in an institution was philosophical rather than contentious. My experience with FEI, the family company, exacted a similar response from me in respect of family companies.

Back I go then to self-employment. I had kept my Dublin and London financial service business ticking over. Part of my deal with Jack was that I could spend a couple of days every month looking after my London clients since I knew that there would be no security working for him. I was in a much healthier state at this point both mentally and financially than I had been when I first branched out on my own. It had been far from easy, that period, and I would have had to dig into a very deep well of courage to face into it again. I resumed my relationship with Ryanair for two or three years, then cashed in my London business and concentrated on building up my Dublin business with the primary purpose of adding enough value in the following ten years to yield a reasonable cash retirement sum. I had lost any pension entitlements I had had, with all the changes of employers, so I contributed as much as cash flow would allow to a pension plan. May and I were not going to have great financial flexibility in our old age, but then when did we ever?

We had moved into our new house in late nineteen eighty-nine so our depleted family (the eldest five had fled the nest) settled back in and I had a nice home to go to when I stopped travelling. In nineteen ninety-four I added a new activity to my existing business. For a number of years there had been increasingly bad publicity for the high street banks in the UK because of questionable application of interest and charges on loan accounts. A number of individuals had devised software packages which were able to replicate the banks' system and these individuals conducted audits which the banks refused to consider. The individuals and their clients went public, producing evidence of malfeasance. Eventually the banks had to climb down and refund significant overcharging. I purchased such a software package from one of the more successful of these individuals, tried it on the Irish system, had it tweaked a bit and set out to offer a bank auditing service to borrowing customers in Ireland. My son Brendan who is a whizz with computers joined me in this activity and after a few wrong turns trying to come to grips with the Irish clearing system we were off.

The nonsense that went on in the banks with regard to the overcharging scandal has been fully aired in all the media outlets. I will therefore confine myself to a selection of those cases where I was directly involved, whether as a 'gamekeeper turned poacher' or a commentator on the attitudes and actions of the banks. The first thing I have to confess is that in the initial stages we made some embarrassing mistakes as we got to grips with the Irish system. Before we realised that it was quite different from the UK system and before we were ready to conduct audits ourselves we got our UK counterpart to conduct an audit on a new corporate client's bank. It was not accurate because of the differences in the two systems and the bank was not slow to rubbish the report. Later we conducted an audit on all the major accounts, loan and deposit, of a busy provincial solicitor's practice. We identified quite a few breaches of contract, presented our report which indicated substantial underpayment and overcharging. But we had overlooked on the deposit accounts the deduction of the dirt tax from interest due. There was still an underpayment after allowing for dirt tax and the overcharge on the borrowings was substantial enough, but the bank mocked us and the client backed away. Those mistakes were not repeated. We became very proficient at doing the audits and over a period of nearly ten years our statistics were: mistakes by the banks to their own benefit 82%, mistakes in the clients favour 2% and 16% neutral or not worth pursuing. If the banks were not cheating they must have set their computers up in such a way that mistakes that favoured the customers would be almost impossible. We all make mistakes but 82% is pretty damning from whatever cause.

One of the biggest refunds we achieved for a client was a six-figure sum. The client had a seven-figure loan at a fixed rate with an early prepayment penalty clause of two percent of the balance. This was unusual because the standard penalty clause stipulated that the customer would be responsible to the bank for any costs arising from the early redemption. This cost would arise only if market rates for the remaining term of the loan were lower than those prevailing when the rate was fixed on the day the loan was drawn down. What you then had was a situation where the bank was paying say, six percent fixed on its own matching funding for the set number of years to the stipulated maturity of the loan, but now they have got the money back and they can lend it out at only say, four percent. Let us say that the loan is one million and there are still three years to maturity. The loss to the bank and the obligation of the customer would be six percent or sixty thousand pounds. The bank conveniently ignored the two percent stipulated in our client's contract and applied the standard contract terms instead. I do not recall the exact amount of the loan or the relevant interest rates but our client had been overcharged one hundred and twenty thousand pounds on this loan. A second loan which we checked for him at the same time, this one at a variable rate, was overcharged by sixty thousand pounds. The bankers said they didn't know how it could have happened. They put up a stern resistance to repaying the one hundred and twenty thousand saying that it was a mistake on their part, a technicality! They had no reply when I asked them if the mistake had been the client's would their attitude remain the same. My client left the talking to me and I became the bankers' number one enemy.

Subsequently they called for another meeting with my client, stipulating that I was excluded. At this meeting they frightened him by saying that I would go public with the story, citing a previous case with the same bank where I did go public without naming names. (That will be the subject of my next case). He settled for one hundred thousand to my chagrin. My fee was a fixed five thousand euro on the penalty overcharge because its discovery took no time, only my expertise, so the settlement he agreed to cost me nothing and him eighty thousand euro. We were on twenty five percent of the sixty thousand overcharge − it was a 'no foal, no fee' contract − and he paid up the two fees totalling twenty thousand promptly.

The contract which did get publicised was as the result of a telephone call I got from RTE Television at a time when I was looking at a cheque for about thirty-three thousand punts from the same bank, payable to my client, which had just come in. The RTE man was trawling in an attempt to establish if all the rumoured overcharging by the banks was a myth. I confirmed that unfortunately it was no myth and at this very instant I was looking at a refund cheque for thirty-three thousand from one of the banks. He pressed for details which I withheld. He then said that he would like to come out to see us with a cameraman and I said "Ok, but I cannot reveal confidential information". He was very persuasive and eventually I agreed to his having the cheque photographed with the name of the payee concealed and a copy of the bank's covering letter, again with the payee's name concealed. Then he said "I have got to produce evidence to my editor and our legal advisor that will support our presentation, so I need a copy of the cheque and the letter". "I can understand your need for authentication but I cannot let these papers out of my office without guarantees that only you, your cameraman, your editor and legal advisor will ever see it". "I give you that guarantee here and now". "On your honour"? "Yes". The cameraman stuck the camera in my face, the reporter asked me a few leading questions and off they rushed for the nine o'clock news. I was only half willing to be manipulated but that reporter had cracked many a harder nut than me.

That evening, there I was for a few seconds on the nine o'clock news, the transaction was aired without any names being mentioned and the following morning it seemed as if the whole country wanted to be clients. Among the calls received there was a ruffled one from my client's accountant, pulling feathers off me for revealing his company's business to the whole of Ireland. It appears that he got a call first thing from a hotshot young reporter from RTE wanting his comments on the bank and the overcharge. He was winding me up a bit (he was an old friend from my Cork days) and he told me with some merriment that one of the owners of the business had just been in to see him. My friend was asked "Could that happen to us"? His reply was "It is us". What I said to the 'honourable' reporter will never appear on the nine o'clock news.

Another incident with a different bank reflected badly on it. I had produced evidence of an overcharge of eleven thousand five hundred punts. When we went to see them the two members of the management were almost foaming at the mouth with hostility to me, and in the end my client and I walked out. Their problem was that up to recently nobody knew enough about the banks' clearing system to tackle them about suspected overcharging and the managers reacted emotionally to anyone who could bring them to book. The client and I agreed that it would be sensible to give them a few days to settle down and he would confront them on his own. When he got there they had had Brendan's figurework properly checked and approved as accurate. The little men then wrote two cheques to the client, one for ten thousand punts and another for one thousand five hundred. They were aware that our fee was based on a percentage of recoveries and they encouraged my client to cheat by suggesting that he could tell me that he settled for fifteen hundred euro if he wished. What but a guilty conscience could have fed such vindictiveness?

I had one final public appearance, post retirement, which did not leave me with happy thoughts. Prime Time had rustled up a retired banker who was prepared to tell the inside story about deliberate overcharging in his bank. He revealed on the programme that at middle management meetings he and his colleagues were encouraged to go out there and cheat the customers. I was going to participate in the show towards the end as an expert commenting on what had been revealed. I spent about two hours sitting in a little cubbyhole of a studio until they got me to say exactly what they wanted. They were out for blood and they did not want to hear anything which would soften the criticism of the banks. Reminding their audience that the abuses they were raising were historic and that things may have moved on, would have given a bit of balance to their accusations. I was prevented from making that point. This was another lesson for me on manipulative TV practices – and they didn't even offer me a cup of tea! Interestingly, when they introduced their version of balance, which was to ask the banks to comment, the Bank of Ireland spokesperson suavely deflected further criticism by declaring that he personally was unaware of such practices and that if on investigation he discovered that these unethical practices did exist he would see to it that they were rooted out. The AIB spokesperson on the contrary did his bank further damage by bristling and spitting out hostile denials. The major whistle-blower was, I think, an ex AIB employee.

As time went on and the banks finally accepted that they had a problem and that operators like Brendan and me were legitimate, they made no fuss and paid up with only cursory checks of the figures. I should have said at the beginning that when we set up our company, Audit Europe Ltd., I went in to the bank where I had had my personal account for some years, to open an account for the company. The young assistant manager was delighted and at my request said he would approve a small overdraft to help get the company on its feet. When I explained what we were doing he abruptly cut the meeting short, saying that I would be hearing from him. We did, and we didn't do business because the bank was the National Irish Bank. It became notorious in nineteen ninety-eight for deliberate overcharging on loan accounts, but it was generally known in the market place long before then that there was an ugly odour emanating from this bank. This gained solidity only when an ex-manager did a whistleblowing job on them to two journalists who published a book on the whole sleazy business. This bank is now a perfectly respectable institution called Danske Bank after its new Danish Parent.

There are only two journalists known personally to me that I could trust during my working life – Bill Tyson of the Irish Independent and Kathy Sheridan of the Irish Times. Kathy Sheridan is such a nice kind person as well as a good journalist. Bill Tyson and I collaborated for a while in an attempt to bring the other bête noir of the Dublin banking scene, Irish Nationwide, to book for its treatment of borrowers.

One of the abuses that Nationwide heaped on unsophisticated borrowers was their misuse of the prepayment penalty to get easy money from customers in difficulty. There was not one person in the company with the courage to suggest that this penalty should not be paid in certain circumstances. Fingleton had them all in thrall. In the case of one couple, under all the pressure they sold off a unit of their land to deal with the arrears. The proceeds of the sale were in excess of the arrears but the company refused to release this excess because the land had been part of their security and releasing the funds would dilute the security cover. It applied the excess to reduction of the loan and slapped a €1700 early repayment penalty on the unfortunate couple. Let me repeat this: they forced the couple to prepay and then charged them for doing so. What a den of moral turpitude!

It was clear long before it happened that Irish Nationwide would come to a bad end. Bad as it was I would never have dreamed that it would have been allowed to behave in such a way over such a long period that it would fold with a cost to the taxpayer of about five billion euro. The Central bank had written to me that it was only interested in the

Nationwide's balance sheet, not the consumer, yet its directors sat on their hands when all the evidence was there of an oncoming disaster. The directors of the ECB also sat on their hands. Nationwide and Anglo Irish Bank, and all the banks to a lesser extent, were in a wild hedonistic orgy of borrowing short and lending long, shovelling money to straw developers, speculators, and over-eager borrowers for residential properties.

Before moving on from Irish Nationwide I should recount another incident that occurred at their 2002 annual general meeting. I was there to highlight the case of the couple above, among others. (I took to the floor and compared Nationwide to a pre-historic monster devouring her young). Someone at the meeting, Brendan Burgess I think, spoke about some of the more noxious actions of the Society, among them the jailing of a client who was having difficulties. MD Fingleton got up and denied that he had ever had anyone jailed. Up shot a client of mine, Joseph Nulty (his name and the incident were reported in the media) to declare that that was funny, he was not long out of jail, sent there at the insistence of Mr Fingleton. I myself was in attendance at the court where Joseph was committed. The judge had asked Nationwide's legal representatives if they wished him to send Mr Nulty to jail and the response was "Yes". I don't think being caught out on a blatant lie disconcerted Fingleton too much. Joseph is my godson and he used to joke with his legal advisor that 'he was going up to Dublin to see 'The Godfather' when things were not going well. His case against the Irish Nationwide is still ongoing.

Involvement in clients' difficulties with Nationwide was a loss leader for me – these people were being hounded by a ruthless and amoral predator for money that they did not have. I was 'giving them a leg up' in so far as I could on the basis that if they got out of their difficulties with a surplus at some time in the future they might share some of it with me. Dealing with clients who were having a problem with the mainstream banks was normally rewarding and demanded much less time and effort. One of my most interesting and amusing cases involved the wife of a client. She called me one morning from up the country and after some preliminary chat she recounted a little anecdote. She and her husband were out socialising the previous evening. The husband had a little too much alcohol and the local bank manager offered to run them home, even though he himself was mildly merry. When they got there the husband offered the manager a fiver 'for the petrol'. The manager, with chuckling indiscretion, said "Ah not at all, sure I've had many a fiver from you that you knew nothing about". The wife's ears pricked up. She was aware of the accusations against the banks in relation to overcharging, she didn't like the man anyway, so the next morning she called me. Sure enough the bank had overcharged them by €28,000. The husband and I had a couple of meetings with the manager and after a lot of humming and hawing the husband agreed to accept €20,000. If it had been left to him he would never have bothered about any overcharging as he and the manager were friendly and he had benefited in the past from that relationship. The wife had wanted her pound of flesh and the next morning my ears were ringing with unkind words because I 'allowed' her husband to compromise!

We had a good record as far as our debtors were concerned. Only two of all the cases we took on reneged on their obligations and their businesses collapsed within a year or two. One of these, a builder, had taken an action for defamation against his bank. Apparently a staff member of the bank made some indiscreet statements in the hearing of other customers which portrayed him as a non-performing borrower. The client suspected that the bank had been overcharging him by a figure in excess of his borrowings. He needed professional confirmation of this so he hired us and another audit practitioner to produce the evidence. We did and the court case proceeded to a successful conclusion. He was awarded over €700,000 and when presented with my bill he refused to pay. I instituted legal proceedings, but after incurring €5,000 in legal charges I was advised not to proceed further. During discovery we identified thirty references in the papers to how critical proving overcharging was to the case. His senior counsel in response to our legal action, then wrote a letter stating that the case was about defamation and only defamation. The senior counsel meantime had been appointed a high court judge and our advice was that no judge would go against the word of a colleague. This lesson about how our legal system works was a costly one for me. I never did find out if my client had chased the bank for the €60,000 overcharge on top of the €700,000-odd defamation award.

The second person who reneged on a €10,000 fee did not refuse to pay as such – he just didn't pay. It was an interesting lesson for me to discover the power of silence. I tried all means, except to knock on the door of his home, to contact this person but failed signally. I called to his office, I telephoned, I wrote letters and sent emails, I wrote to his solicitors – all I got was silence! There was no chance that I was going down the legal route again, so he got away with it.

Towards the end of the nineties business began to wind down slightly as the banks slowly regrouped and made some attempt to eradicate illegal overcharging. Brendan went off to an outside job and Marie Masterson, who had been my secretary/PA previously, took on the computer work. I retired from all activities in 2004 on my seventieth birthday and devoted more time to golf and gardening.

I have written much about my footballing activities and mentioned in passing my interest in golf but I haven't alluded at all to my real interest – gardening. From my earliest days watching my father planting trees in Ballinvalley of the stone walls and rock art, I have had a strong interest in trees. This developed over time into almost a passion for gardening. The fact that it also contributed hugely to my continued fitness after retiring from football was a bonus.

When we moved from Cork to Dunshaughlin in 1976, I planted eleven hundred trees on the garden boundaries. With the exceptional fertility of the local soil they grew very quickly, providing shelter for less hardy shrubs and flowers and now, abundant firewood. What I liked most of all was the artistic aspect of creating a harmonious restful space. Over time the garden has taken on many different personalities. Now it's a wild and natural place, which gives me great pleasure and takes less maintenance.

The Wild Garden

A colourful section of the front garden pre-retirement

The Ponds c.2002

EPILOGUE

My race is run now, I am enjoying good health in my golden years and I have many moments of reflection on my past life. I have done many good things in life, but I am sometimes uncomfortable about some which I wish I had done differently or not at all. However, I get some comfort from the thought that one can only work with what one has got, and to expect perfection from an imperfect human being would only lead to disappointment and perhaps depression. I also console myself with the thought that I have always tried to behave with goodwill and a sense of honour towards others. When my failings have hurt or disappointed others it is a matter for regret, but life is for living and dwelling on such things will not change them. Maya Angelou wrote "You may not control all events that happen to you, but you can decide not to be reduced by them." I have not coasted through life – there have been too many really difficult and character-forming experiences for that to be true. However, I have been blessed with a character and attitude which has enabled me to give the rough times a Gallic shrug and to face a sometimes uncertain future with courage and humour. "The Child is father of the Man" – it was the young carefree boy roaming the countryside barefooted around Sliabh na Callaigh, giving up his hard-earned weeks wages at a simple request of his mother, snagging turnips on a cold November day, being thumped by a ram and tossed by an ass, who made me the man that I was.

Now, in my eightieth year I get up every morning on death row but I couldn't care a hoot. Only good memories remain and I revel in the loving support of a large family. Many of my grandchildren are close by to keep me cheerful and to bring wonder again into my life. I awake every morning thankful to see another day and face it with cheerful optimism. I would like to depart this life like my Uncle Pee. He was bent over tying his bootlaces for another exciting day when he expired.

"It's not the years in your life that count, it's the life in your years".

Dunshaughlin Tuites

The SWATs – Stuck With a Tuite [or TOPs – Tuites on Purpose]
Aisling, Joanne, Laura, Des, Costas, May, Willem; Dee & Annika

Some Grandchildren

Emily, Alex, Donagh, Ally, Anton; Sadhbh, Aoife, Elena, Rory, Rebecca;
Oisín & Sinéad, Seana, Duana & Fiachra, Patrick & Isaac

More Grandchildren

Maeve, Peter, Ailbhe, Tiarnan, Meera, Rohan, Dara, Muireann, Aibhín

Swedish Great-grandchildren – Milea Kathleen and Colin

Friends and Family at my 80th birthday